Partners in Peace and Education

Roman Catholic–Presbyterian/Reformed Consultation IV
Text and Discussion Guide

Edited by

Ronald C. White, Jr., and Eugene J. Fisher

WILLIAM B. EERDMANS PUBLISHING COMPANY
GRAND RAPIDS, MICHIGAN

Copyright © 1988 by Wm. B. Eerdmans Publishing Co.
255 Jefferson Ave. S.E., Grand Rapids, Mich. 49503

Library of Congress Cataloging-in-Publication Data:

Roman Catholic-Presbyterian / Reformed Consultation.
Partners in peace and education / Roman Catholic-Presbyterian / Reformed Bilateral
Consultation;
edited by Ronald C. White, Jr. and Eugene J. Fisher.
p.   cm.
Bibliography: p. 136
ISBN 0-8028-0346-6
1. Peace—Religious aspects—Christianity.
2. Arms race—Religious aspects—Christianity.
3. Church and education—United States.
4. Church and state—United States.
I. White, Ronald C. (Ronald Cedric), 1939-
II. Fisher, Eugene J.
III. Title.
BT736.4.R66 1988
261.8'73'08822—dc19   88-6948
                                             CIP

Contents

PERSPECTIVES ON EDUCATION, THE STATE, AND RELIGION

Preface

Partners in Peace and Education is the document worked out by Round IV of the Roman Catholic-Presbyterian/Reformed Consultation jointly sponsored by the Bishops' Committee for Ecumenical and Interreligious Affairs of the National Conference of Catholic Bishops and the Caribbean and North American Area Council of the World Alliance of Reformed Churches (Presbyterian and Congregational). This American dialogue between the two confessional traditions has been going on uninterruptedly since 1965. The reports of Rounds II and III were printed in book form in *The Unity We Seek* (Paulist Press, 1977) and *Ethics and the Search for Christian Unity* (I. A Statement on Abortion; II. A Statement on Human Rights; USCC Publications, 1980) respectively. Documents previously published were either in book form (*Reconsiderations* [1967]) or printed in church periodicals with reprints available (*Ministry in the Church, Women in the Church, Recommendations for Changes Regarding Inter-Christian Marriages* [1971]).

In the present Round IV the approved main theme was "An Ecumenical Approach to the Relationship of Church and State." We started out from the topic "The Church and the Kingdom of God" of the international Roman Catholic/Presbyterian-Reformed dialogue. The task that gradually emerged was to explore the relation of Kingdom and Church with reference to problems confronting American society today. So the final title became "The Church and the Kingdom: Church—State—Society." Our consultation focused on two topics: Church and Nuclear Warfare, and Church and School.

Under the first topic, the consultation examined the Bishops' Pastoral Letter of 1983 together with statements on peace and nuclear warfare of the various Presbyterian and Reformed churches. While acknowledging the state's legitimate use of coercive power, the participants unanimously emphasized that nuclear war is morally intolerable and that nuclear deterrents must lead to disarmament. Worthy of mentioning is a remark made by a Reformed participant in regard to the Pastoral Letter; he said that "this is the first time that Reformed groups have endorsed a Catholic document for their own internal use" (thousands of copies were sent to Presbyterian congregations).

Looking into the relationship of Church and State, participants discussed a wide scope of issues beginning with the establishment clause. A Roman Catholic participant, while analyzing the First Amendment, remarked, "I dismiss the fable that the original founders sought to remove religion from the public sphere; rather, they sought to disestablish religion."

It was acknowledged that both traditions have a strong commitment to education. The religious neutrality in U.S. public schools was a common concern; it was agreed that education about religion should play a more prominent role in American public schools.

Divergence in particular policy judgments was squarely presented, such as tax relief for parents of children enrolled in religiously sponsored schools. The quality of the argumentation, however, was clearly shown when the consultation pointed to the need that proponents of both positions must carefully assess the roots of the differences: are they theological or historical-sociological?

In addition to the consultation document we present in this volume some of the background papers to give the readers a glimpse into our "workshop" as we mutually instructed, enlightened, and inspired each other.

Beside the actual statements of the document, we have—as in previous Rounds—some underlying motives, which were further strengthened in our present consultation. We wanted to prove that the accusation of so many frustrated ecumenists that the ecumenical movement has lost its momentum was not true, at least not with us. Also, we confronted another charge (made lately by Fr. Thomas Stransky in America) that "the bulk of formal dialogues has been concentrating on everything but ethical issues" that may be very divisive for the churches today. We can say in good conscience that our consultation, particularly in the last three Rounds, has been deeply engaged in examining the ethical implications of the confronting issues.

The more we work together in these consultations the more we find the true meaning of unity not in uniformity but by learning to view the heritage of our respective traditions (and of other Christian churches as well) and thus to appreciate the richness and the beauty of them as God's precious gift. As Avery Dulles puts it: "It would be most unfortunate if the ecumenical imperative meant that the separate Christian traditions had nothing better to do than to die" ("Pluralism—A Gift to the Church," *AT/ONE/MENT* [March 1986]: 3).

We want to continue what we feel is our commission. The two parent bodies (Bishops' Committee and World Alliance Area Council) have already approved Round V and its general theme: Laity in Church and Society; the Changing Perception of Discipleship.

Until then and then again we want to preserve the spirit of our consultation: we have been and want to be a family of brothers and sisters in Christ. The Word of Jesus about the Good Shepherd characterizes our ideal. John 10:16 says "And I have other sheep that are not of this fold . . . they will heed my voice. So there shall be one flock, one shepherd." We may well be of two different folds. But we do not want to look at each other with jealousy or hostility. Rather, we want to discover on each others' faces the glow of love that looks forward to the Good Shepherd's face and hears his voice. Here is our unity we seek, there the unity we find.

BISHOP ANDREW HARSANYI
BISHOP ERNEST UNTERKOEFLER

Introduction

This small volume is an invitation to partnership. In the fresh winds of the Spirit that have been blowing since Vatican II, Christians of differing traditions have been discovering their unity in Christ. The partners are meeting each other in various ways and in different places.

The focus of this conversation between fellow believers is peace and education. For three and a half years official representatives of the Roman Catholic and Presbyterian-Reformed traditions met together in what is called a bilateral consultation. One result of their reflection, inquiry, and debate is an official document that forms the heart of this book. But a larger fruit is the hope that individuals and parishes will continue the conversation in living rooms and parish halls across the country. The subject matter carries with it its own urgency in these critical days. The vitality of these two traditions, both so important in the shaping of this nation, now are open toward each other as never before.

When you are together we believe you will join in some of our discoveries. For some of us this was our first experience with this kind of intentional dialogue. As such we found ourselves surprised again and again by the common faith that flowed between us. At times we found ourselves on different sides of an issue—but the sides were often not between delegations but within delegations.

The process of our official bilateral consultation was to meet twice a year, a total of seven meetings in all. Each time we met for three days with papers prepared to guide our discussions. We met alternately at Princeton Theological Seminary and at retreat centers in Washington, D.C. Our fifth session was held in Charleston, South Carolina, at the residence of Bishop Unterkoefler of the Catholic diocese of Charleston.

We discovered, as we hope you will, that the quality of our reflections and conversation increased with the quality of our fellowship. In retrospect the meeting in Charleston was a turning point both in terms of the candor of discussion and the enthusiasm for the getting of this project into the hands of the people of our churches.

In putting together this volume we have decided to augment the

official document in three ways. We are publishing representative official peace documents of the member Presbyterian-Reformed churches
and the official summary and excerpts from the 1983 statement of the
Catholic bishops, *The Challenge of Peace,* to enrich the discussion on
peace. We are presenting here also three papers on education edited for
this volume. Finally, we are including study questions as a guide to
meetings between Catholic and Reformed groups. These questions are
meant to be suggestive but not exhaustive. They are divided into weekly
sessions, but we realize that your own format may dictate other time
patterns. Our only encouragement is to give yourself enough time—one
meeting will not do—to get to know each other and the issues.

In our own official dialogue as we went deeper into an issue, we
discovered that although we were arriving at similar places we got there
by quite different routes. At one point in discussions about peace, representatives from the Reformed tradition were speaking about the propensity of the nation for both good and evil. We referred back to the Reformed Church in America peace document and its dependence on
recent biblical scholarship on the Pauline use of the principalities and
powers. Several Catholics picked up on the same issue but spoke to it
from the biblical teaching on creation as well as the tradition of natural
law, which itself has biblical origins in the Wisdom tradition. It was at
this and many other points that we became self-conscious both about
our own traditions and the traditions of others.

But partners do not just arrive at the same point in a journey. We
also learned to express our disagreements. Certainly this is so in the
whole conversation about education. None of us can step away from
long histories in America that have given shape to present positions—
and prejudices. But even here the story is not one of unanimity within
traditions. The Christian Reformed Church offers a different model
within the Reformed tradition.

But how do partners disagree? With clarity, fervor, and respect.
And appreciation. If at first we may have been polite in our disagreements, we came to discover that the more we knew each other the more
we could speak out of our deepest heart about matters important to us.
A discovery that may be yours is that the presence of those from a different tradition may help you clarify your own position. The value of
being in a study group with persons of a Catholic parish or a United
Church of Christ congregation will come when someone asks: "What
do you mean by that?"

One of the things we learned in our discussions may also be of help to your group when questions of meaning emerge. This is the reality that the Catholic and Presbyterian-Reformed communities have had differing experiences in the past in this country. When Catholics tell their "family stories" in America, they will often speak of the experience of immigration into a predominately Protestant society, and of suffering religious and ethnic discrimination. Presbyterian and Reformed, while also being immigrants, do not always have the same memory of those experiences. Such memories, of course, help to shape the way we approach various issues that face us all today.

Likewise, the experiences of our two traditions in Europe after the Protestant Reformation have differed, so that some of our shared religious vocabulary, whether in liturgical piety or concerning our understandings of the relationship of church to society can have quite distinct nuances to each of us. To paraphrase the famous dictum of Augustine, we must be willing to "have mercy upon words" in dealing with one another in dialogue.

These differences, seen within the common perspective of our shared Christianity, can greatly enrich our understandings not only of each other but, equally important, of ourselves. In debunking the myths we may hold about each other, and in learning from each other new ways to appreciate ancient truths, we enlarge our understanding of the one truth we are called upon by our common baptism to seek and to proclaim. Whenever Christians gather for ecumenical dialogue, our own experience over the past several years leads us to affirm, the Spirit is present.

When historians look back on the twentieth century they may well call it the ecumenical century. Christians of various traditions are coming to know each other after four hundred years of separation. But to be ecumenical is not to forget the traditions that have nourished us. What is the distinctive contribution that Christians of Catholic persuasion can make to the church and the world? What is the distinctive contribution that Christians of Reformed persuasion can make? We can come to know ourselves and our family better in this kind of conversation. We do not give up but rather add to as we come together.

We would appreciate your using the tear-off page at the back of the book to give us feedback on both the book and the process. In this publication we are concerned to put down a historical record of a consultation concluded, but we also want to help launch a conversation that can grow in the coming years.

RONALD C. WHITE, JR.
EUGENE J. FISHER

Participants

Roman Catholic

JAMES T. BURTCHAELL, a Holy Cross priest, is professor of theology at the University of Notre Dame. Educated at Notre Dame, the Gregorian University in Rome, Catholic University in Washington, and the Ecole Biblique in Jerusalem, he earned his doctorate at Cambridge University. His interests include Christian ethics and systematic and pastoral theology. It was during his service as Notre Dame's provost that he became a spokesman for national associations of independent and Catholic universities on First Amendment issues.

EUGENE J. FISHER is on the staff of the Bishops' Committee for Ecumenical and Interreligious Affairs of the National Conference of Catholic Bishops. He has degrees from the University of Detroit and New York University. He is the author and editor of numerous books, including *Faith Without Prejudice* and *Twenty Years of Jewish-Catholic Relations*. In 1981 he was named by Pope John Paul II consultor to the Holy See's Commission for Religious Relations with the Jews, and in 1985 he was appointed a member of the International Catholic-Jewish Liaison Committee.

DANIEL J. HARRINGTON is a Jesuit priest and professor of New Testament at Weston School of Theology. He was president of the Catholic Biblical Association in 1985–86. He has been general editor of *New Testament Abstracts* since 1972. His most recent books are *The New Testament: A Bibliography* and *Targum Jonathan of the Former Prophets*.

MONICA F. HELLWIG is a lay member of the Catholic church and professor of theology at Georgetown University. She has done social work, counseling, broadcasting, and ghost-writing at the Holy See. She is involved in conferences, retreats, and workshops for church groups in the United states and abroad. Her publications include *Understanding Catholicism, Jesus, The Compassion of God*, and *Christian Women in a Troubled World*.

WILLIAM J. HILL is a Dominican priest and professor of systematic theology at the Catholic University of America. From 1975 to 1983 he was editor-in-chief of the *Thomist*, and currently serves on the editorial board of the *New Catholic Encyclopedia*. His publications include *Knowing the Unknown God* and *The Three-Personed God*.

JOHN T. PAWLIKOWSKI is a Servite priest and professor of social ethics at the Catholic Theological Union in Chicago. He serves on the Catholic Bishops' Advisory Committee for Catholic-Jewish Relations and the National Council of Churches' Christian-Jewish Relations Standing Committee. His publications include *Biblical and Theological Foundations of the Challenge of Peace* and *Justice in the Marketplace*.

GERARD S. SLOYAN is a priest of the Diocese of Trenton and professor of religion at Temple University. He previously taught at the Catholic University of America. Before participating in this dialogue he was a member of two successive bilateral consultations with United Methodists. He is the author and editor of many publications, the most recent being a commentary on John in the Interpretation series.

ERNEST L. UNTERKOEFLER was installed in 1965 as the tenth bishop of Charleston. He has served as a pastor in Virginia and auxiliary bishop of Richmond. He has served as chairman of the Bishops' Committee for Ecumenical and Interreligious Affairs. Among his publications he was editor of *The Unity We Seek* and *The American Catholic Church and the Negro Problem in the XVIII–XIX Centuries*. He has served as co-chairman of the Roman Catholic/Presbyterian-Reformed Consultation since 1967.

Presbyterian/Reformed

DOROTHY DODGE is a Presbyterian elder who teaches political science at Macalester College. She served as a member of her denomination's peace-making task force that helped produce the document included in this volume, "Peacemaking: The Believer's Calling." Her publications include *African Politics* and *Continuities and Discontinuities in Political Thought*.

ANDREW HARSANYI, a native of Hungary, is a bishop in the Hungarian Reformed Church in America. He has served as curator of books on the Reformation in the National Library of Budapest. After 1945 he cared for Hungarian refugees in Austria. In the United States he has served Presbyterian congregations as well as an American-Hungarian bilingual Reformed church. His publications include *The Black Friars in South Eastern Europe before the Reformation*. A member of the consultation since its beginning in 1965, he has been co-chairman since 1972.

ANNE EWING HICKEY is an ordained Presbyterian minister living in Louisville, Kentucky. She holds a Ph.D. in religion from Vanderbilt University. She has taught at Louisville Presbyterian Theological Seminary and at Bellarmine College. Her publications include *Women of the Roman Aristocracy as Christian Monastics*.

ELIZABETH JOHNSON is an ordained Presbyterian minister and assistant professor of New Testament at New Brunswick Theological Seminary. She holds a Ph.D. in New Testament from Princeton Theological Seminary. Her dissertation is "The Function of Apocalyptic and Wisdom Traditions in Romans 9–11." She served for four years as chaplain and instructor in humanities at Queens College in Charlotte, North Carolina.

CORNELIUS PLANTINGA is an ordained minister of the Christian Reformed Church and associate professor of systematic theology at Calvin Theological Seminary. He has degrees from Calvin College, Calvin Seminary, Yale University, and Princeton Theological Seminary. He is the author of three books, including *A Sure Thing*.

MAX L. STACKHOUSE is an ordained minister of the United Church of Christ and the Herbert Gezork Professor of Christian Social Ethics and Stewardship Studies at Andover Newton Theological School. He served as president of the Society of Christian Ethics for 1986–87. He works closely with the United Church Board for World Ministries, the National Council of Churches, and the Association of Theological Schools on questions of church and society. His recent publications include *Creeds, Society, and Human Rights* and *Public Theology and Political Economy*.

RONALD STONE is an ordained Presbyterian elder and professor of social ethics at Pittsburgh Theological Seminary. His special teaching areas are urban church and society, political and economic ethics, and peacemaking and international affairs. His publications include *Reformed Faith and Politics* and *The Peacemaking Struggle: Militarism and Resistance* (Dana Wilbanks, co-editor).

ROBERT A. WHITE is an ordained minister of the Reformed Church in America and president of New Brunswick Theological Seminary. He has served two pastorates and, as Minister for Social Witness, directed denominational programs for peacemaking, hunger education, and social action. He is co-author of *Christ is Our Peace: Biblical Foundations for Peacemaking* and author of the study document "Christian Faith and the Nuclear Arms Race" included in this volume.

RONALD C. WHITE, JR., is an ordained Presbyterian minister. He is director of continuing education, lecturer in church history, and editor of the *Princeton Seminary Bulletin* at Princeton Theological Seminary. He has served as a parish minister, college chaplain, and college, university, and seminary teacher. His publications include *The Social Gospel: Religion and Reform in Changing America* and *American Christianity: A Case Approach*.

Partners
in Peace
and Education

In 1980, the sponsors of the consultation, the National Conference of Catholic Bishops' Committee on Ecumenical and Interreligious Affairs, and the Caribbean and North American Area Council of the World Alliance of Reformed Churches, approved the main theme of Round IV of these continuing bilateral consultations. The theme was an ecumenical approach to the relationship of church and state. The steering committee of the consultation refined this definition and determined that we should explore "The Church and the Kingdom: Church—State—Society."

The first part of our document ("Theological Context") considers our common biblical and patristic heritage on these matters, and describes points of agreement and disagreement in Catholic and Presbyterian/Reformed theologies on issues of kingdom, church and state. Then as a way of exploring further these theological perspectives, we have focused on two topics relating church and state in contemporary American society: the peril of nuclear warfare ("Church and Nuclear Warfare") and the role of government in matters of education ("Church and School").

Theological Context

Whenever Christians from divided traditions take up the complex questions of the relations between kingdom, church and state, they find, as we have, that sooner or later their discussions must be tested against the witness of Scripture. From the very beginning, Scripture proclaims the sovereignty of God over all creation, tells how the practical consequences of God's reign were made manifest at Sinai, and traces the history of God's covenant and the people's often imperfect attempts at respecting God's sovereignty. Ancient Israel's experience of God led it both to recognize the importance of social realities for religious life and to insist, as the prophets did, on the relative character of every social and political institution in the light of God's reign. As the story of God's

1

people proceeds, the "kingdom of God" is gradually revealed to refer to God's future display of power and judgment, to the future moment when all creation will acknowledge God's rule and when the promises to God's people will be fulfilled. Jesus, as heir to the tradition of Jewish law, prophecy and wisdom, has taught us also to look for anticipations of God's kingdom in the present. The life, death and resurrection of Jesus shine forth as the dramatic anticipation of the fullness of God's reign. In the present the kingdom confronts us as God's constant rule, sovereignty and loving dominion.

The church is in principle the community of those who believe in Jesus Christ and his proclamation of God's kingdom. It preserves the spirit of Jesus and tries to be faithful to it. It prays and yearns for the fullness of the kingdom and works in service of the kingdom. It lives its life against the horizon of the kingdom. It is the sign and symbol of hope for the fullness of God's kingdom in the future. It announces the kingdom and encourages God's people to live in accord with the standards of the kingdom, though it cannot claim to be the fullness of the kingdom. The early church had much in common with Jewish and Greco-Roman groups of its time; what set it apart from them was its faith in the power of Jesus' death and resurrection as God's decisive self-disclosure in human history and decisive inauguration of the fullness of the kingdom.

The early Christians knew what it means to be a minority with respect to state and society. Through his proclamation of the kingdom of God, Jesus challenged assumptions of his society and so came into conflict with religious and political leaders. This challenge led to his death at the hands of the governmental officials.

Neither Jesus nor his first-century followers were in a position to influence directly the political and military policies of the Roman Empire. Nor could they transform immediately the cultural and moral attitudes of the peoples around them. Their general policy toward the empire was acceptance and even cooperation (see Mark 12:13-17 par.; Rom. 13:1-7; 1 Pet. 2:13-17), resisting only when the state interfered unjustly in their religious lives (see Acts 5:27-32; Rev. 17). The early Christians did not negate political life any more than they negated family or economic life; they relativized it. That is, they saw that membership in the kingdom and in the church meant that political and governmental authority was not ultimate and could not finally save humanity.

Over time, the extension of this principle eventuated in notions of government as not absolute. The early Christians' missionary strategy was to share the good news of God's kingdom anticipated in Jesus and to show by their good example what a difference the good news could make in their everyday lives. Yet even the cautious steps in the New Testament give some hints about the Gospel's power to influence governments and transform lives. In the changing circumstances of the church throughout history, there have been moments of great success on the church's part and times of great failure in these tasks.

History has taught us to beware of all claims identifying the kingdom with particular political, social, or ecclesiastical structures. However, it has also shown the danger of an exclusively future, otherworldly or individualistic understanding of the coming kingdom. God's full exercise of the divine reign over creation involves radical conversion of human hearts, relationships and social structures, and thus is a process of redemption going on in the course of history. This is a work of divine initiative welcomed and implemented within human freedom.

As representatives of the Catholic and Presbyterian/Reformed traditions in the United States of America in the late 20th century, we have greater opportunities and responsibilities with respect to our government and our society than the early Christians had. We are also more directly involved in the difficult task of discerning when the church must say yes to the state and when it must say no. For all the faults of this society, and they are many, Christians in this land are grateful for the theological ancestors who struggled to preserve a society in which religious people can influence popular consciousness, change laws, organize communities and exercise political power. Many of our brothers and sisters in other lands are not nearly so fortunate in their opportunities to affect state and society. As Christians, we understand our political and public activities as flowing from our commitment to God's kingdom and church. We wish neither to neglect our responsibilities to our fellow citizens (and to the world) nor to reduce our faith to merely political action.

From the earliest days of American history, Presbyterian/Reformed Christians have been prominent in shaping our state and society. Viewing the commonwealth as an imperfect but anticipatory expression of God's kingdom, Presbyterian/Reformed Christians have undertaken political and public activities as grateful and obedient responses to God's call. They have taught all of us about reforming society through laws, the need for voluntary associations, respect for human wisdom, the formulation of just standards and their applications, the regulation of political systems, checks and balances, and the separation of church and state. In the midst of these positive activities, Presbyterian/Reformed Christians have never ceased recalling the ambiguity of political and public activities on account of their roots in fallen human nature.

Since the settlement of Maryland in 1634, Catholics in America have also developed a spirit of pluralism and toleration, one which over time allowed selective but highly significant embracing of principles also held by Reformed Christians on public matters. Catholics have made important contributions in enabling various immigrant groups to participate responsibly in American society, in developing labor unions and in energizing urban politics. For various historical reasons, American Catholics have been somewhat less prominent than Presbyterian/Reformed Christians in shaping our governmental and social institutions. That situation has changed, however, and the full range of political and social opportunities and responsibilities is now open to most American Catholics. This development coincided with the renewal of biblical studies in the Catholic Church, Vatican II's declarations on religious freedom *(Dignitatis Humanae)* and the church in the modern world *(Gaudium et Spes),* and the theological re-evaluation of the venerable tradition of natural law.

The time is ripe for American representatives of the Catholic and Presbyterian/Reformed traditions to express their common theological understanding of kingdom, church and state, and to explore what this means with regard to some highly sensitive issues facing American society and what it means for our shared hopes for Christians in communion.

The long traditions of the Catholic and Presbyterian/Reformed churches, both when they were united in one communion from the early church through the late Middle Ages and since their division in the West into discrete bodies, agree on many aspects of a theological frame of reference regarding kingdom, church and state. They agree that not only the communities of faith rooted in Jesus Christ but also the political orders of the world exist in relation to the kingdom of God. That is, they understand church, society and state to exist under the rule of God and governed by the laws of God; they live toward the ends and purposes of reconciliation, peace and justice for all humanity; and they bear within them, at least in partial ways, the marks and clues of the kingdom as it is already at work in history.

With this understanding the churches have the fundamental responsibility to identify, preach, teach and exemplify the power of this kingdom and, on this basis, call all members of society to responsible participation in church and political life. Failure to acknowledge or heed these laws leads to disaster and destruction. Society has priority, and the state is a temporal institution organized to protect society and the church. To put it another way, the kingdom may find its marks not only in the church but also in some aspects of society, even if rarely in any state.

The churches have a vocation to preach, teach and exemplify by word, sacrament and deed the promises and the present power of divine life in the world. Their efforts at improving the quality of human life here and now are signs of their faith in God's promise to bring about the fullness of the kingdom. They try to facilitate the social reign of God in all aspects of civilization, insofar as this is possible within the limits of human history. The Christian tradition asserts that political authorities and institutions likewise have a responsibility under God both to protect the freedom of religious bodies to fulfill their vocation and to order the structures of social life in accord with the common good.

There is a necessary distinction between church and state. Christians maintain that the church's existence and goal derive from God in Christ, not from human efforts or historical conditions alone. The modern state has immense powers of taxation, regulation, judicial determination and administration, all reinforced by coercive power. The churches in the United States work in society without these powers. Governance in the state may require the use of coercive power, especially in controlling illegitimate violence and securing justice, whereas the church violates its own nature when it relies on such coercion as an instrument in ensuring obedience to its laws and ends. Moreover, the church is committed to values and principles that extend to all humanity, whereas the state is inevitably focused on the interests and well-being of the nation.

The church also supports, guides and defends the rights of institutions in society not directly controlled by the state—families, schools, unions, hospitals and various community organizations—so that state coercive powers can never become the sole comprehensive determinant for social policy. The use of coercive power must always be limited.

Political authority must be guided by concern for the preservation and improvement of all non-governmental institutions. State power must serve the society and all humanity, not simply control them.

As American Christians today, we are discovering that we share a common biblical heritage, a common set of opportunities and responsibilities, and a common theological framework. We are also discovering that we share the task of discerning when to speak the prophetic word of the Gospel to our government and our society. Nevertheless, some real differences in approach and expression remain. As a way of understanding these differences, while acknowledging the great progress already made toward theological convergence, we have focused on two issues: how our churches speak to American government and society, and how American government and society shape and sometimes subvert our churches. In exploring the first issue, we have focused on official statements by our churches regarding nuclear warfare. In investigating the second issue, we have looked especially at legal rulings regarding state aid to church schools and related matters. On nuclear warfare, our conclusions are similar but our ways of approach and expression differ. On the second issue both our conclusions and our approaches differ somewhat (though not strictly along denominational lines).

Church and Nuclear Warfare

Since this round of the consultation began, the U.S. Catholic bishops have discussed, revised and finally approved their pastoral letter on war and peace, titled "The Challenge of Peace: God's Promise and Our Response." During this time, nearly all of the related Reformed and Presbyterian denominations have also debated and passed statements regarding Christian responsibilities as we face the growing perils of nuclear warfare and international political-military confrontation. In both the Catholic and Presbyterian/Reformed treatments of these matters, key issues about church and state, and about Christian understandings of kingdom, society and political life generally have been central. More and more of our bilateral conversations focused on issues of church and state especially as they involve the use and the limits of coercive power in and by political authority in the context of the present nuclear perils. Thus, our discussions were conducted with a sense of urgency and with a desire to find agreement wherever possible.

It was frequently and widely acknowledged in our discussions that the U.S. Catholic bishops' pastoral letter on war and peace is one of the most discerning and prophetic statements on the issue in recent years. In terms of both its substance and its impact on public discourse, this letter may well do for this issue in the American context what Martin Luther King, Jr., did for the issues of racism: the conscience of the nation, and not only that of a specific communion, is given a new level of cogent expression by religious leadership. Several of the Presbyterian/Reformed national bodies have endorsed this letter and commend it to their congregations for study along with the various denominational statements. This signals a new level of joint witness to the society by the churches which exceeded our original expectations and encouraged the further work of our bilateral consultations.

In our consultations we have studied various Presbyterian/Reformed statements on war and peace along with the pastoral letter and a series of discerning background papers written by the participants. We explored the history of our traditions, both as churches separated from one another and as heirs of a common history prior to the Reformation, and have been made aware again of the spiritual, moral and political dangers of a too-intimate relationship between piety and coercive force. We confess that both our traditions have at times violated Christian principles and damaged political justice in this regard. Yet because religion and politics seem inevitably to influence one another, past errors are no reason to avoid confrontation with the problems anew. Indeed, the awareness of dangers to church and to state when these relationships are false or ill-considered prompts us to deepen and broaden our dialogue, and to identify questions needing greater clarity. The following are key questions that emerged from the discussions and from study of the various documents.

In modern life, the instruments of coercive power reach devastating proportions. The traditional vocation of the church to see that the use of military power be restrained is intensified. Churches are called to see that "common good" extends beyond national boundaries to all humanity and to see that temporal power remains constrained by universal moral principles. All believers and communions who share this heritage are to give regular and sustained witness to those principles which promote peace. Political authorities are to conduct their responsibilities so that the prospects for peace are increased. The churches have the responsibility to teach and clarify the principles of moral life in such a way that the citizenry, especially those who are members of the churches, can exercise the duties of citizenship with moral and spiritual discernment.

The discussion of church-state issues, in the context of the various denominational positions on war and peace in our nuclear age, indicates that common emphases, stated somewhat differently in different branches of our churches, have their characteristic theological groundings and particular implications.

The core logic of the bishop's pastoral letter, like that of the Presbyterian/Reformed statements, uses a combination of arguments from Scripture, from the traditional discussions of just war theory and from social-ethical analysis of the contemporary situation. These communions of the Christian family recognize that there are strong impulses toward non-violence in the New Testament and that it is a primary duty of Christians to be peacemakers. Both communions recognize that in political affairs the limited use of coercive power may be required in order to maintain civil order, protect the neighbor from arbitrary violence and serve the common good. In contrast to some Christian communions, both the Roman Catholic and Presbyterian/Reformed traditions have held over the centuries that it is possible to be a Christian soldier or magistrate. In other words, one may be a faithful communicant and exercise coercive power—or even participate in some kinds of war as a conscientious combatant. That is to say that although there is always a pressure toward non-violence in these traditions, unqualified pacifism is not the only ethical posture for the Christian. It may be the vocation of some.

In the historic traditions of these two communions of Christianity, the arguments justifying this common stance have been somewhat different. The Western Catholic tradition, for the most part, has been dependent on criteria for reluctant but justifiable uses of coercive power developed by Augustine and others under the somewhat confusing heading "the just war theory." The phrase does not mean that war is just. It reflects the encounter of Christianity with complex political civilizations in which Christians are also citizens and magistrates. Distinctions between justifiable and unjustifiable uses of coercive activity by political authority have to be made.

The Presbyterian/Reformed churches share much of the heritage that derives from the days of the old Roman Empire. Often they also articulate the "just war" criteria as guidelines for believers. More often, however, they turn to the Old Testament and see analogies between the responsibilities placed by God upon the Israelites to engage in battle for justice and righteousness' sake, and the responsibilities of Christians to see that governments do not exploit innocent and defenseless peoples or prevent the people from worshiping God. The perils of state idolatry and quest for ultimate security in military response to crises are also frequently accented.

The two modes of argument are quite similar in result and allow for considerable convergence in our ethical witness in society. Yet some differences of note remain. The Catholic tradition modulates the tendencies of some to read the New Testament in absolutist ways by placing a high value on the faithfulness of church leaders who attempted to apply New Testament motifs to a complex Roman civilization and thereby produced an authoritative "tradition." The Presbyterian/Reformed churches tend to rely more on the Hebrew Scriptures and the application of these biblical accents to modern civilizations.

Both ways of working tend to put the pacifist tendencies of some New Testament passages into a larger historical, ethical, and civilizational context of interpretation, although the different historical and civilizational understandings bring about distinctive styles of ethical judgment as the Gospel is related to complex socio-political problems. For example, the Catholic tradition draws heavily on principles adopted into canon law or promulgated by official pronouncements by councils and popes. Presbyterian/Reformed traditions, by contrast, often utilize biblical phrases, such as Christ's disarming of the "principalities and powers" (Eph. 6:12) to state analogous principles. Both communions tend to disagree with those traditions which see pacifism as the only response of a Christian, and call for responsible Christian engagement in political life, even as it may require the use of coercive means, as a proper vocation of magistrate and citizen. Both communions see peacemaking as a mandate of a Christ-informed conscience and community.

At moments in the past, individuals or groups in both the Catholic and Presbyterian/Reformed churches have misappropriated both tradition and Scripture in ways that have turned "just war" and biblical analogies to "holy war," that is, into legitimations of morally unjustifiable "crusade." At such moments the New Testament witness toward non-violence has been obscured or forgotten. In the pastoral letter and in the current Presbyterian/Reformed statements, efforts are now being made to recover and retain that witness, not in a way that excludes or denies the legitimacy of limited coercive power as a necessary instrument of the state but as a governing priority which should be set forth as the norm of those who live under and toward the kingdom.

The new urgency of nuclear confrontation has evoked a more holistic reappropriation of the heritage. The pacifists and those who recognize the states' right to defensive war under certain conditons unite in denouncing nuclear war. Preparation for nuclear war is morally intolerable. Nuclear deterrence must be transformed into nuclear cooperation and disarmament.

Non-violent, peaceful human cooperation is the law and purpose of God. The burden of moral proof rests on those who use armed force, even the state. Peace within a state requires justice. States have no right to ignore justice and to defend particular governments with a reign of terror under the claims of national security. Nor do superpowers have the right to intervene in neighboring states to thwart domestic struggles for social change under the banners of national interest or national security. There is growing agreement that justifiable revolutions, such as certain "wars of liberation," also come under these terms and have to bear the burden of proof. Even these can never become unqualified "holy war."

These matters are worth noting in the context of the discussion of church and state. They reveal that these two communions of the Christian family have a similar understanding. Neither believes Christianity requires disengagement from problems of power in civilization; and neither can allow "reasons of state" such as "national interest" or "defense security" or even "liberation" to become sovereign over conscience or society. Christians, we hold in common, live in the real world of power politics, but the norms of political life come from Christian ethics founded in Scripture, church tradition and reason. The latter must form and inform the former.

The above motifs lead us to a second point of comparison and contrast. The United Presbyterian Church statements and the United Church of Christ statements, particularly, accent a theme also strongly present in the Catholic pastoral letter: Christians are to be peacemakers, and the peace that is to be made by faithful and obedient action is *shalom*—a "just peace" that reflects spiritual joy. "Peace" is not simply the absence of violent conflicts, but involves both structures of justice and the realizing of spiritual wholeness. This peace disarms structures of oppression and destruction both in the institutions of society and in the human heart.

Several Presbyterian/Reformed bodies affirm that peace cannot be achieved by ending the arms race unless there is economic reform, extension of human rights to those now denied them, the establishment of democratic political institutions and the liberation of minorities, women and Third World peoples in all areas of ecclesiastical, social and civil life. Comparable motifs can be found in Catholic opinion, particularly in the papal encyclicals of the last hundred years. But there is also a stronger emphasis in the Catholic tradition on that dimension of peace which has to do with the inner, spiritual cultivation of the response to God. To be sure, this is present in several of the Presbyterian/Reformed contributions to our consultations, but it is less overt. This is an area where convergence is probably necessary to have a fully catholic, fully evangelical, fully reformed and fully orthodox community of faith. Nothing in either tradition inhibits convergence at this point. All seem to be aware that without real social justice and without inner spirituality lasting peace is unlikely even if we avoid the immediate perils of pending nuclear destruction.

One way in which the church is distinguished from the state is that it knows that "justice," as a precondition of peace, is ultimately rooted in that form of spirituality which brings "joy" and empowers persons to become peacemakers. The church also knows that spirituality of this sort has the best chance to flourish and grow where injustice does not stunt human development and force people to attend only to the struggle of survival. Justice and joy require one another as mutual preconditions to *shalom*.

In the Presbyterian/Reformed discussions of the bishops' pastoral letter a very important point emerged that has many implications for our topic. It was a series of scattered, but substantial and enthusiastic comments about the way in which the pastoral letter was developed. The process whereby the letter moved from early proposals to final draft involved open hearings with Protestant as well as Catholic theological and ethical scholars, circulation of several drafts with open invitations for comment, discussions with laity in government and defense, experts in political and nuclear affairs, and discussion at congregational levels.

The sensitive inclusion of diverse opinion, especially as it involves openness to the "ministries" and insights of laity, appears to many Reformed and Presbyterian members to be a "post–Vatican II" indicator of possible convergence in the understanding of authority and polity in the churches. Not only has this helped overcome some of the authoritarian stereotypes by which many Presbyterian and Reformed Christians tend to view Catholic ecclesiology, but it seems to have implications for the whole church's role in the shaping of conscience on political affairs.

In this connection the mode of address of the bishops' letter is to Catholics, to other Christians and to all those who seek a world free of nuclear threat. It is not in the first instance a statement directly to the U.S. government—although there are many indications that governmental leadership was quite interested in how the discussions came out. Policy-makers in American political and military affairs were not ignored nor are the more concrete political judgments to which these documents come binding in all their detail.

What is presumed by the documents on nuclear armaments by Catholics and Presbyterian/Reformed alike is that a committed, informed and ethically secure population will work through democratic channels to see that morally questionable policies will be modified. Such a presumption will seem unremarkable to a great number of people. In the context of critical Catholic and Presbyterian/Reformed reflections on church and state, the implications are significant.

Church leadership has a responsibility to work with and through the people. The people have the responsibility to use their informed consciences to shape the use of political and military power. Persuasion and the authority of the word in preaching and teaching operate through the consciences of the people, who will then see that political authority (including that which determines military policy) is the servant and not the master of human existence. To be sure, all are "to be obedient to the governing authorities" (see Rom. 13:1-7), but when authorities become a terror to good, the people through free discussion, persuasion and open democratic processes may—indeed, must—see that these policies or the leadership promulgating them are altered.

It is possible to identify some of the main theological motifs that lie behind our discussions of church and state with reference to the specific crisis of nuclear peril:

1. Creation is a gift of God. Even if it is tainted with sin since the Fall, it is not to be destroyed by an armaments contrived by human persons. No political or military policy which portends devastation of the

world can be approved by the church, whatever political philosophies
and interests may be involved.

2. The churches are called not only to see that creation is regarded
but to contribute to redemption from the Fall and its effects, even
though every church has fallen elements within it. The church is able
to do this because the kingdom of God is over, beyond and in the
church. The methods of the church are primarily by preaching, teaching and sacrament, and by social action, social service and political engagement. Rightly understood, these are never merely political and
never without spiritual-moral content with political implications. The
ministries of the church transcend national boundaries, representing an
international community seeking peace.

3. The state is an instrument of society and must serve humanity.
Every political order or government involves the possible use of coercive, even lethal, power to protect and preserve human societies. In
those moments when the state brings about the conditions which allow
freedom, justice, joy and peace, the state may serve God's redemptive
purposes. Participation in political life as responsible citizens or leaders
is a high office to be honored and encouraged. When political authorities or structures become more destructive than preservative and redemptive, Christians may withdraw their obedience to clearly unjust
civil laws and conscientiously engage in civil disobedience, being
willing to suffer prosecution by the state for the sake of reforming state
policy and bringing its law to accord with a just order. Should this civil
disobedience and active non-violence fail and the state respond only
with arbitrary violence and perpetuation or increase of an unjust order,
the state may well forfeit its claim to legitimate governance. It may become, instead, a highly organized rebellion against right order, just
peace and the common good. Then Christian citizens may commit
themselves to the reconstruction of a preservative and redemptive
government by the use of force against the rebellion of officials mask-
ing as a government.

4. Christians live in church and society in hope. The eschatological awareness brought by the threat of nuclear apocalypse invites us to
act for *shalom* in the face of despair. We know that only God can bring
the fulfillment of the kingdom promise and deliver us from the perils
we have made for ourselves. Yet by grace we place ourselves under
God, as people of God, to be witnesses to and servants of the purposes
of God in the world. In all that we do, therefore, we bring our faith and

our theology, our love experienced in Christian fellowship and from Christ, to the realistic analysis of political and military questions that we may actualize our hopes for the kingdom of God wisely.

On these matters, we agree and urge all in our member churches to work more closely together to make these motives active in this land. Whatever other differences and divisions remain and will remain for a time, these common elements of witness on church, state and peace are points of convergence to be celebrated at local, pastoral, regional, national and international levels and, we pray, also in heaven.

Church and School

Education was a second area in which we tested our understandings of kingdom, church and state in the American context. As our discussion progressed, we realized that we were treating different, although related, issues: policies of the churches and of the government with regard to education generally, religiously sponsored schools and the place of religion in the public schools. These issues entail, naturally, church attitudes and influences on governmental policies in education and the ways in which governmental policies permit, enhance, or inhibit the capacities of the churches to follow the mandates of their faiths. Before those issues can be addressed directly, it is necessary to identify some presuppositions about the nature of education according to our religious traditions. It is also important to define the terms of our discussions.

Both the Catholic and the Presbyterian/Reformed traditions have strong commitments to education in theory and practice. Both traditions encourage education as a service to the mind and its gifts, helping young men and women to understand this world and themselves. As Christians we esteem education as one way of enhancing our readiness for the kingdom and for union with the Lord. With faith as motivation and perspective, education can lead us to appreciate this world as God's creation and to learn how to live and serve one another here as companions. We both stress the importance of education as a necessary instrument enabling persons to fulfill their vocations, to participate as good citizens in their society and to contribute to the common good.

Both the Catholic and the Presbyterian/Reformed traditions view religion as penetrating all areas of life and so look on all areas of life as religiously significant. Therefore, all human studies and scientific endeavors are to be conducted with deep regard for the most profound moral and spiritual values necessary to human well-being. Moreover, all education must be conducted with the recognition that religious and ethical questions may well be involved in the selection, presentation and evaluation of such materials. Because of the intimate relationship of knowing and believing, and of ethics and preparing for life, both traditions look on teaching as an especially significant vocation; they encourage people to undertake teaching as a profession; and they promote learning and study as a lifelong activity. Historically these traditions have been among the leading founders of schools, colleges and universities. Of special significance to both traditions is the nature and character of the early stages of education which, we hold, must foster a sacred regard for truth, a love of humanity, a principled view of morality and justice, a personal commitment to responsible labor, community life, civility and culture.

While we have rejoiced in discovering our common enthusiasm for and commitment to education, we have also noted points at which our perspectives regarding kingdom, church and society may lead us to differ on educational matters and on public-policy questions that influence education. Acknowledging the great investments that both traditions have made in higher education, we have nevertheless focused our conversations on the more sensitive areas of primary and secondary education. We have talked chiefly about grades 1 through 12; that is, the period in which most states in the United States have stipulated a legal obligation for children to attend school (at least to the age of 16). Most children fulfill this obligation within the state-sponsored or public school system. All taxpayers must support this system even if their own children do not attend or even if they have no children at all. It is against the U.S. Constitution, as interpreted by the Supreme Court, to use the public school curriculum or resources to propagate or show preference to any specific religion. Although the historical, literary, cultural and philosophical study of religion is permitted, the common, although dubious, interpretation of the separation of church and state makes such study rare. Thus most American children attend state-sponsored schools which are funded by all taxpayers and which are not only prevented from promoting any particular religion but which avoid those permitted treatments of religion which are surely necessary for a complete education.

Some American children attend schools under the direction of religious bodies (diocese, religious orders, parishes, denominations, judicatories, congregations, etc.). The Catholic primary and secondary school system consists of approximately 9,500 schools and serves over 3 million students. Few Presbyterian/Reformed churches in the United States sponsor schools. In this respect, however, the Christian Reformed parent societies have been a notable exception. Evangelical Protestant schools, some connected to the Presbyterian or Reformed traditions, are growing rapidly; in the last three years, they are being founded at the rate of about 300 per year. The religiously sponsored schools generally give preference to members of their own churches, but many welcome children from other (or no) religious backgrounds, and some use their private, parochial, or diocesan systems to provide quality education to disadvantaged groups where public systems are weak. From the legal perspective, the state must treat religiously sponsored schools in the same way that it treats private independent secular schools. Catholic schools include about half of the total number of teachers and 56 percent of the students enrolled in U.S. non-public, all-day schools.

Christians in America have had their own distinctive motivation for founding religiously affiliated schools. The impartiality of the U.S. Constitution has been applied to government-sponsored schools by obliging them to be neutral toward religion. That has caused difficulties for some Christians in many traditions. At various times and places this requirement has not been honored, and parents found their children subjected to what they regarded as objectionable sectarian influences by teachers. And when neutrality was enforced, parents found that when matters of great importance were being taught, the elimination of religious viewpoints and teaching, while all other viewpoints (including those opposed by believers) were set forth, left pupils at a disadvantage. Only in religiously committed schools, they concluded, could the full range of the believer's mind and interests be freely explored, with the benefit of the Christian community's insight and wisdom.

Within this context we have discussed a number of controversial issues. On some questions we find much agreement; on others we tend to divide by communion; and on still others we find agreements and disagreements that do not neatly follow our particular traditional divisions. For example, we tend to agree that a state-authored prayer, to be offered in the public schools, is not to be recommended on either religious or constitutional grounds. Not only must the rights of minorities be protected but government bodies are seldom theologically competent for performing the task which belongs to churches and families and individuals. Further, we agree that while the government has a right and a duty to support public education, it is important that provisions which allow tax-free, non-profit private and religious schools to exist and to develop patterns of education outside of or beyond those provided for by the common purse be sustained, provided only that they meet health, safety and minimal academic standards proper for government to protect. And we tend to agree that when it is deemed unnecessary or impossible for children who are religious or come from religious families to attend religiously sponsored schools, churches must provide supplementary programs to prepare the youth for faithful adulthood. Finally, we agree that teaching "about" religion is constitutionally possible, important for a holistic educational experience, and too seldom carried out. Children who are not exposed to the great faith traditions of the world with at least as much objectivity and detail as they are now exposed to economic and political ideologies, to artistic perspectives, and to scientific theories and hypotheses are educationally deprived.

On one issue, however, we tend to disagree according to whether we are rooted in the Catholic or the Presbyterian/Reformed traditions, although there are exceptions even here. Most striking in this regard is the sensitive question of whether government at the national, state, or local levels should provide some form of tax relief, direct aid, or subsidy for parents to use in the education of their children if the parents decide to send their children to a private or religiously sponsored school.

This current and much-debated issue is a concrete way of exploring similarities and differences in Catholic and Presbyterian/Reformed approaches to education in the context of our theologies of kingdom, church and state. It is important to observe at the outset that we are stating common, perhaps even majority, viewpoints, but not monolithic or unanimous opinions of all our church members or leaders.

With that caution stated, it is fair to say that many Catholics and some Presbyterian/Reformed Christians (especially members of the Christian Reformed Church) argue that the government should provide tax relief for parents of children enrolled in religiously sponsored schools. The following are arguments in favor of such tax relief:

1. Parents have the primary responsibility for educating their children, though they may require the help of the state in certain aspects of education. The principle of subsidiarity suggests that tax relief would

increase the freedom of parents in educating their children with the least interference in the precise mode and content of education.

2. At present, parents pay for both the public schools through their taxes and the religiously sponsored schools through their tuitions and contributions. As a matter of equity, many argue, parents deserve and need such tax relief as a just response to this double burden.

3. The proposed tax relief, parental aid, or subsidy may be understood to be a transaction between the government and the parents, and not one directly between the government and the church or between the government and the religiously sponsored schools.

4. The consequence would be the pluralization of educational efforts and would encourage innovation in educational designs according to the particular needs of the students and their families. In this pluralism, religiously sponsored schools could develop even better forms of education in explicitly religious atmospheres. Students would be encouraged to relate their studies more directly to their faith commitments, and the benefits of a richly pluralistic society would be more widely gained.

Most Presbyterians, many Reformed Christians, and some Catholics oppose tax relief for parents of those enrolled in religious and other private schools. The following are arguments against such tax relief:

1. The education of the next generation is a responsibility of all the citizenry and is best effected through public schools in a democratic society. Parents may have special faith commitments that require the right to organize schools outside of the publicly provided systems of education, but the public has no responsibility to subsidize, directly or indirectly, these special commitments.

2. Such tax relief, aid to parents, or subsidy are in fact devices to bypass present prohibitions against entanglement of the government in religiously sponsored education and would, in effect, promote the religious bodies that sponsor the schools. It is therefore a violation of the Constitution.

3. Such proposals might well reduce commitment to the common good in sustaining quality public schools both by diverting funds from public education and even more by eroding the concern among the voting population to commit major tax dollars to public schools. The public schools could become underfunded custodial institutions for those segments of the population which have the least resources, financially, emotionally, politically and institutionally.

4. Pluralism in educational design and program may more easily and equitably be worked out through modification of present public school curricula, etc., without promoting a pluralism which tends to segregate faith communities during the formative years of education. In this connection the churches must promote responsible participation in the common problems of the education of our youth and insist on quality of instruction "about" religion in the public schools without detracting from the specific vocations of churches and families, and trying to get schools to do their jobs for them.

The Catholic approach to this issue is based on the individual's right to an education, the primacy of the parents in educating their children and the principle of subsidiarity whereby the larger unit of the common life, the state, supplements the efforts of parents to carry out their tasks. The Presbyterian/Reformed approach, where it conflicts with the Catholic one on this issue, is based on the duty of all the citizenry to provide quality education for the next generation through common institutions and democratic participation, on a firm adherence to the separation of church and state in form and consequence, and on a vision of the church as a witness within public institutions and structures rather than the architect of private alternatives.

Both traditions affirm that religion permeates every facet of life. They differ with regard to what is the best way of educating children and to recognize and appreciate this reality—through the total environment of the religiously sponsored school or through the public school as supplemented and given a religious framework by the church? Both traditions agree that parents bear the primary weight of the public's responsibility for educating children. They differ on the role that the state should play in the educational process—promoting the education of youth as a subsidiary to parents and church or primary provider of education for most children? Both traditions affirm that freedom and justice are involved in this issue. The usual Catholic position is that tax relief is a matter of justice that would enhance the freedom of parents. A frequent Presbyterian/Reformed position argues that not using the public schools is a free choice for which parents should be willing to pay, and that equality of opportunity and quality of education are best provided by the common public administration of the schools.

A major historical factor in leading Catholics in the United States to develop their own school system was the perception that the public schools in some areas at least were rooted in Protestantism and promoting Protestant values. Even then, however, there was an articulate body of support for Catholics being educated in public schools and thus bringing about a change in the ethos of those schools. At a later period, some Protestants called for the disentanglement of public schools from all religious doctrines or observances, in part out of fear that the growing Catholic population might impose its own religious program on the public schools.

Today Catholics and Presbyterian/Reformed Christians are probably more concerned about the alleged neutrality of the public schools toward religion. Our discussions have indicated how widely the public schools in certain geographical areas vary with regard to religion. Depending on the administration and faculty and on the religious atmosphere of the community, the local public school may be perceived as friendly or hostile toward religion. The official policy, however, is neutrality. The same discussions have raised the questions of religious people about this alleged neutrality: Does neutrality lead to disregard for religion as a historical and cultural force? Does neutrality suggest that religion is not very important? Does neutrality hasten the process of secularization and even promote so-called secular humanism?

The religious neutrality of the public school is the context in which most American Catholic and Presbyterian/Reformed children are educated. Even though the American Catholic Church is strongly committed to its religious school system, the Catholic Church assumes that governments may establish their own schools insofar as the common good requires them. Since the vast majority of Catholic students in the United States attend public schools, there is naturally strong support for and influence on the public school system by Catholic parents. Moreover, the Catholic Church encourages Catholics who teach in public schools to give a good example of their religious commitment and Catholic students to share their faith with others. Presbyterian/Reformed Christians look upon the public schools as offering an experience of pluralism that prepares children for adult life in the United States. Both communions affirm that religious people—teachers and students—make important contributions to American society through their presence and participation in public schools. We wonder whether it would be good for our society and for our churches if all children of religious parents were studying in religiously sponsored schools. Such a situation might deprive our public schools of any religious presence and might marginalize our churches with respect to the larger society.

Our churches see the need to supplement, integrate and at times correct public school education with explicitly Christian education. The most obvious supplement is the religious education program sponsored by local congregations. Some churches also provide remedial help for public school students through various tutoring programs. There are always practical problems regarding the limited amount of time available for religious education and the quality of the programs that are available. The principles, however, are that all Christians have a right to a Christian education, that parents have the primary responsibility for assuring and providing such an education, and that our churches must make available an education enabling children to relate their faith to the materials and experiences comprising the rest of their educational program. Our two traditions doubt that the study of life, the world and human thought can be fully enriching and complete without awareness that these are to be understood in the context of God's law, God's purposes and God's love, and without recognition that the people of God have the responsibility to proclaim the kingdom of God in all areas of human existence, including education. We are untrue to our theological traditions if we fail to show our children how faith can be integrated into their everyday lives.

Public schools have been the ground on which intense political and legal debates regarding church and state have taken place. These debates concern prayer in public schools, teaching about religion in public schools, the access of religious groups to public school facilities and the rights of public schools to provide sex education and so-called values clarification. While there is not much vocal opposition to prayer in public schools from our churches, there is not much positive enthusiasm for the idea either. Too many Catholic adults recall readings from a "Protestant" Bible and the recitation of "Protestant" prayers; too many Presbyterian/Reformed Christians fear the inroads of fundamentalism.

Teaching about religion in public schools is a new phenomenon in the United States. Our concern is the manner in which it is done: The presentation should be as accurate and objective as possible, without giving the impression that religion is irrelevant or outdated, while not promoting any one religious perspective. The question of the access of religious groups to public school facilities depends on the circumstances of use (time, nature of the activity, etc.). Here our discussion tended to divide on familiar grounds, with Catholics arguing that justice required such access to all taxpayers, and Presbyterian/Reformed participants expressing caution about entanglement and state promotion of religion.

The right of public schools to provide sex education is accepted (with some reservation) by both traditions. The reservation is that this sex education be positive, accurate and prudent, guided throughout by fundamental ethical principles necessary to the formation of personal responsibility and viable relationships in all sexual behavior. Our traditions agree that sex is never, for humans, simply a matter of physiology or even of psychology. We agree that human sexuality involves moral and spiritual values at every point, and that, according to the teachings of both our traditions, sexual activity is to be carried out in the context of stable, loving, monogamous, heterosexual relationships that are sacramental or covenantal in character. Insofar as these perspectives are not allowed or emphasized in sex education courses in the public schools, tension will remain between them and the churches. Catholic and Presbyterian/Reformed Christians disagree among themselves on particular moral judgments regarding sexual matters, but combine in declaring that sexuality is of profound moral significance.

A similar problem arises with regard to "values clarification" or "values education." We agree that it is important to clarify values, but we also agree that the values held by people, once clarified, need to be evaluated. And that requires the recognition and articulation of things that are basically and "objectively" right and good. Neither of our traditions will be satisfied with values clarification which denies the possibility of discussing such ethical matters, as much of current values clarification seems to. Whose values will be taught? Will these values be Christian or religious? Will they be inimical to religion?

Our conversations about church and school have made us aware of our common commitment to education, our differing approaches to church-and-state relationships in the American context, and the challenges we share in transmitting religious values to the next generation.

Challenges Ahead

Our conversations on the kingdom-church-state relationship have sharpened our consciousness of the biblical and theological framework we share on these matters. They have also made us aware of the opportunities and responsibilities facing us as committed Christians in the

United States who seek to be both good citizens and faithful to our religious commitments.

A. Reflection on our churches' official statements about nuclear warfare has revealed that we can reach similar conclusions on the basis of similar theological underpinnings (about creation, kingdom, church and state) by somewhat different theological emphases (biblical teachings, "just war" criteria) and in different literary forms (the varied and concise Presbyterian/Reformed statements, the massive letter of the U.S. Catholic bishops).

It should also be noted that there is a growing acceptance of non-violent options in Catholic circles similar to non-violent trends in Presbyterian/Reformed churches. In addition, there is a deepening reliance on the biblical tradition within the Catholic community as a whole. On the other hand, there is increasing interest in some Presbyterian/Reformed circles in the interpretation of the classical "just war" theory.

Study of one another's statements on the nuclear issue leads us to offer the following suggestions:

1. Catholic and Presbyterian/Reformed Christians should be encouraged to read one another's official statements on the nuclear issue (and indeed on other issues also). Attention to their differing emphases, methods and literary forms is enlightening and can promote ecumenical understanding.

2. These statements also challenge our churches to reflect on the positive nature of the peace that we seek and perhaps come to a more holistic vision of peace (social, personal, spiritual, etc.).

3. As religious people in the United States, we must make our fellow citizens more conscious of the nuclear danger and find creative ways of influencing the political process toward just peace through global reconciliation.

4. We strongly recommend to our respective denominations that other churches be consulted, their representatives be integrated into the drafting process and that wherever feasible we speak together in joint official statements on peace and other major social issues.

B. Consideration of issues related to education has increased awareness of our common commitment to education. Our theological traditions have impelled us to encourage Christians to embrace education and even to found schools, colleges and universities. In the American context, we share perspectives on certain issues: the right of private schools to exist, the value of religiously oriented people in public schools, the importance of learning about religion, wariness regarding government-authored or government-imposed prayers, etc. Our conversations on the education issue lead us to the following suggestions:

1. The matter of tax relief brings forward deeply felt and powerful attitudes regarding church and state. There is need for proponents of both positions to listen carefully. Presbyterian/Reformed Christians need to understand why American Catholics have been so reluctant to accept the state as the adequate or exclusive provider of education. Catholics need to understand better why Presbyterian/Reformed Christians are so vigilant about government entanglement in religion. Both of us must assess the roots of our differences: Are they theological or historical-sociological? Is change possible?

2. There is also serious need for religious people to reflect across denominational lines on what their participation or non-participation in public schools may mean. The major issues for such reflection include the nature of Christian witness in American society, the kind of religious education needed to supplement, integrate or correct the academic program, the appropriate attitudes toward specific issues (school prayer, access to facilities, sex education, values clarification), and the implications for the larger society, especially for the poor, of any weakening of communal commitment to the welfare of the public schools.

3. In the course of our discussion on the church and state-supported schools, we have recognized the growing power of forces in contemporary American society that directly or indirectly would render religious values and hence religious education peripheral at best to an authentic sense of human existence. This is especially true with respect to those institutions that shape our popular culture. While there is no consensus among us on how best to deal with these disturbing trends (e.g., by improving programs in public schools, increased commitment to church schools, more effective integrative efforts), we are convinced that joint discussions of this critical feature of American public life must continue in earnest in the days ahead.

Conclusion

Our allegiances to church and to state are stressful; they are not divided. We do not see the church as presiding over God's claim on us, while the state is left to manage the affairs of this world. We do not construe the one as inward, the other as outward. We do not yield to either a governance over the other. We believe and we hope in the conformity of ourselves, as individuals and as a people, to the loving rule of God— the kingdom—through the way we live and interact within these two societies.

The United States of America has afforded us Christians almost unprecedented freedom to proclaim our faith, to worship as we choose and to enjoy immunity from civil control or taxation. Our attitude toward the state, however, goes well beyond mere appreciation for this liberty. It is in the public order that we fulfill the Lord's relentless call to feed, house, clothe, heal, defend and, in every needed way, to sustain our sisters and brothers. Our energetic participation in the civil state and its policies and institutions is an indispensable sequel to our love of neighbor for the love of God.

And here arises the stress. It is right, we claim, for us to act as citizens in the political order on the strength of the perspectives and criticism that our religious faith affords us. Our review of the debate over warfare and nuclear arms has reinforced our conviction that we will not have our religious judgments disallowed in the public forum. It is only as Christians that we properly and fully understand the peace we seek in the civil order. We have not accepted the liberty to believe as we will at the price of cloistering those beliefs in the privacy of the church. We cannot be faithful Americans except as publicly and articulately Christian. And the peace movement has been a particular reminder to us that ecumenical collaboration yields not only political alliances, but a re-possessed understanding of Jesus' call that makes us better believers, better citizens.

There is another stress. Precisely because the decisions of state bear so heavily on human welfare which we see to be of eternal significance and because our American civil government is constrained from submitting to the doctrine of any church, we Christians are inveterately distrustful of yielding much authority to state control in matters of the mind and conscience.

We conclude with a blessed irony. What is most remarkably congenial to the Christian churches in American civil policy is due partly to persons and to philosophies that were hardly Christian. Yet it is only if we are most reflectively and pragmatically Christian that we, in the Catholic and Presbyterian/Reformed churches, will contribute most as American citizens. Thus may we serve the coming of the kingdom.

Church Peace Documents

Summary of "The Challenge of Peace: God's Promise and Our Response"

National Conference of Catholic Bishops

May 3, 1983

The Second Vatican Council opened its evaluation of modern warfare with the statement: "The whole human race faces a moment of supreme crisis in its advance toward maturity." We agree with the council's assessment; the crisis of the moment is embodied in the threat which nuclear weapons pose for the world and much that we hold dear in the world. We have seen and felt the effects of the crisis of the nuclear age in the lives of people we serve. Nuclear weaponry has drastically changed the nature of warfare, and the arms race poses a threat to human life and human civilization which is without precedent.

We write this letter from the perspective of Catholic faith. Faith does not insulate us from the daily challenges of life but intensifies our desire to address them precisely in light of the gospel which has come to us in the person of the risen Christ. Through the resources of faith and reason we desire in this letter to provide hope for people in our day and direction toward a world freed of the nuclear threat.

As Catholic bishops we write this letter as an exercise of our teaching ministry. The Catholic tradition on war and peace is a long and complex one; it stretches from the Sermon on the Mount to the statements of Pope John Paul II. We wish to explore and explain the resources of the moral-religious teaching and to apply it to specific questions of our day. In doing this we realize, and we want readers of this letter to recognize, that not all statements in this letter have the same moral authority. At times we state universally binding moral principles found in the teaching of the Church; at other times the pastoral letter makes specific applications, observations and recommendations which allow for diversity of opinion on the part of those who assess the factual data of a situation differently. However, we expect Catholics to give our moral judgments serious consideration when they are forming their own views on specific problems.

The experience of preparing this letter has manifested to us the range of strongly held opinion in the Catholic community on questions of fact and judgment concerning issues of war and peace. We urge mutual respect among individuals and groups in the Church as this letter is analyzed and discussed. Obviously, as bishops, we believe that such differences should be expressed within the framework of Catholic moral teaching. We need in the Church not only conviction and commitment but also civility and charity.

While this letter is addressed principally to the Catholic community, we want it to make a contribution to the wider public debate in our country on the dangers and dilemmas of the nuclear age. Our contribution will not be primarily technical or political, but we are convinced that there is no satisfactory answer to the human problems of the nuclear age which fails to consider the moral and religious dimensions of the questions we face.

Although we speak in our own name, as Catholic bishops of the Church in the United States, we have been conscious in the preparation of this letter of the consequences our teaching will have not only for the United States but for other nations as well. One important expression of this awareness has been the consultation we have had, by correspondence and in an important meeting held at the Vatican (January 18-19, 1983), with representatives of European bishops' conferences. This consultation with bishops of other countries, and, of course, with the Holy See, has been very helpful to us.

Catholic teaching has always understood peace in positive terms. In the words of Pope John Paul II: "Peace is not just the absence of war. . . . Like a cathedral, peace must be constructed patiently and with unshakable faith" (Coventry, England, 1982). Peace is the fruit of order. Order in human society must be shaped on the basis of respect for the transcendence of God and the unique dignity of each person, understood in terms of freedom, justice, truth and love. To avoid war in our day we must be intent on building peace in an increasingly interdependent world. In Part III of this letter we set forth a positive vision of peace and the demands such a vision makes on diplomacy, national policy, and personal choices.

While pursuing peace incessantly, it is also necessary to limit the use of force in a world comprised of nation states, faced with common problems but devoid of an adequate international political authority. Keeping the peace in the nuclear age is a moral and political imperative. In Parts I and II of this letter we set forth both the principles of Catholic teaching on war and a series of judgments, based on these principles, about concrete policies. In making these judgments we speak as moral teachers, not as technical experts.

I. Some Principles, Norms and Premises of Catholic Teaching

A. *On War*

1. Catholic teaching begins in every case with a presumption against war and for peaceful settlement of disputes. In exceptional cases, determined by the moral principles of the just-war tradition, some uses of force are permitted.

2. Every nation has a right and duty to defend itself against unjust aggression.

3. Offensive war of any kind is not morally justifiable.

4. It is never permitted to direct nuclear or conventional weapons to "the indiscriminate destruction of whole cities or vast areas with their populations . . ." (*Pastoral Constitution*, #80). The intentional killing of innocent civilians or non-combatants is always wrong.

5. Even defensive response to unjust attack can cause destruction which violates the principle of proportionality, going far beyond the limits of legitimate defense. This judgment is particularly important when assessing planned use of nuclear weapons. No defensive strategy, nuclear or conventional, which exceeds the limits of proportionality is morally permissible.

B. *On Deterrence*

1. "In current conditions 'deterrence' based on balance, certainly not as an end in itself but as a step on the way toward a progressive disarmament, may still be judged morally acceptable. Nonetheless, in order to ensure peace, it is indispensable not to be satisfied with this

minimum which is always susceptible to the real danger of explosion"
(Pope John Paul II, "Message to U.N. Special Session on Disarmament," #8, June 1982).

2. No *use* of nuclear weapons which would violate the principles
of discrimination or proportionality may be *intended* in a strategy of deterrence. The moral demands of Catholic teaching require resolute
willingness not to intend or to do moral evil even to save our own lives
or the lives of those we love.

3. Deterrence is not an adequate strategy as a long-term basis for
peace; it is a transitional strategy justifiable only in conjunction with
resolute determination to pursue arms control and disarmament. We are
convinced that "the fundamental principle on which our present peace
depends must be replaced by another, which declares that the true and
solid peace of nations consists not in equality of arms but in mutual trust
alone" (Pope John XXIII, *Peace on Earth*, #113).

C. The Arms Race and Disarmament

1. The arms race is one of the greatest curses on the human race;
it is to be condemned as a danger, an act of aggression against the poor,
and a folly which does not provide the security it promises. (Cf. *Pastoral Constitution, #81, Statement of the Holy See to the United Nations, 1976.*)

2. Negotiations must be pursued in every reasonable form possible;
they should be governed by the "demand that the arms race should
cease; that the stockpiles which exist in various countries should be re-
duced equally and simultaneously by the parties concerned; that nuclear weapons should be banned; and that a general agreement should
eventually be reached about progressive disarmament and an effective
method of control" (Pope John XXIII, *Peace on Earth*, #112).

D. On Personal Conscience

1. *Military Service:* "All those who enter the military service in
loyalty to their country should look upon themselves as the custodians
of the security and freedom of their fellow countrymen; and when they
carry out their duty properly, they are contributing to the maintenance
of peace" (*Pastoral Constitution*, #79).

2. *Conscientious Objection:* "Moreover, it seems just that laws
should make humane provision for the case of conscientious objectors

who refuse to carry arms, provided they accept some other form of community service" (*Pastoral Constitution,* #79).

3. *Non-violence:* "In this same spirit we cannot but express our admiration for all who forego the use of violence to vindicate their rights and resort to other means of defense which are available to weaker parties, provided it can be done without harm to the rights and duties of others and of the community" (*Pastoral Constitution,* #78).

4. *Citizens and Conscience:* "Once again we deem it opportune to remind our children of their duty to take an active part in public life, and to contribute towards the attainment of the common good of the entire human family as well as to that of their own political community. . . . In other words, it is necessary that human beings, in the intimacy of their own consciences, should so live and act in their temporal lives as to create a synthesis between scientific, technical and professional elements on the one hand, and spiritual values on the other" (Pope John XXIII, *Peace on Earth,* #146, 150).

II. Moral Principles and Policy Choices

As bishops in the United States, assessing the concrete circumstances of our society, we have made a number of observations and recommendations in the process of applying moral principles to specific policy choices.

A. On the Use of Nuclear Weapons

1. *Counter Population Use:* Under no circumstances may nuclear weapons or other instruments of mass slaughter be used for the purpose of destroying population centers or other predominantly civilian targets. Retaliatory action which would indiscriminately and disproportionately take many wholly innocent lives, lives of people who are in no way responsible for reckless actions of their government, must also be condemned.

2. *The Initiation of Nuclear War:* We do not perceive any situation in which the deliberate initiation of nuclear war, on however restricted a scale, can be morally justified. Non-nuclear attacks by another state must be resisted by other than nuclear means. Therefore, a serious moral obligation exists to develop non-nuclear defensive strategies as rapidly as possible. In this letter we urge NATO to move rapidly toward the adoption of a "no first use" policy, but we recognize this will take

time to implement and will require the development of an adequate alternative defense posture.

3. *Limited Nuclear War:* Our examination of the various arguments on this question makes us highly skeptical about the real meaning of "limited." One of the criteria of the just-war teaching is that there must be a reasonable hope of success in bringing about justice and peace. We must ask whether such a reasonable hope can exist once nuclear weapons have been exchanged. The burden of proof remains on those who assert that meaningful limitation is possible. In our view the first imperative is to prevent any use of nuclear weapons and we hope that leaders will resist the notion that nuclear conflict can be limited, contained or won in any traditional sense.

B. On Deterrence

In concert with the evaluation provided by Pope John Paul II, we have arrived at a strictly conditional moral acceptance of deterrence. In this letter we have outlined criteria and recommendations which indicate the meaning of conditional acceptance of deterrence policy. We cannot consider such a policy adequate as a long-term basis for peace.

C. On Promoting Peace

1. We support immediate, bilateral verifiable agreements to halt the testing, production and deployment of new nuclear weapons systems. This recommendation is not to be identified with any specific political initiative.

2. We support efforts to achieve deep cuts in the arsenals of both superpowers; efforts should concentrate first on systems which threaten the retaliatory forces of either major power.

3. We support early and successful conclusion of negotiations of a comprehensive test ban treaty.

4. We urge new efforts to prevent the spread of nuclear weapons in the world, and to control the conventional arms race, particularly the conventional arms trade.

5. We support, in an increasingly interdependent world, political and economic policies designed to protect human dignity and to promote the human rights of every person, especially the least among us. In this regard, we call for the establishment of some form of global authority adequate to the needs of the international common good.

This letter includes many judgments from the perspective of ethics, politics and strategy needed to speak concretely and correctly to the "moment of supreme crisis" identified by Vatican II. We stress again that readers should be aware, as we have been, of the distinction between our statement of moral principles and of official Church teaching and our application of these to concrete issues. We urge that special care be taken not to use passages out of context; neither should brief portions of this document be cited to support positions it does not intend to convey or which are not truly in accord with the spirit of its teaching.

In concluding this summary we respond to two key questions often asked about this pastoral letter.

Why do we address these matters fraught with such complexity, controversy and passion? We speak as pastors, not politicians. We are teachers, not technicians. We cannot avoid our responsibility to lift up the moral dimensions of the choices before our world and nation. The nuclear age is an era of moral as well as physical danger. We are the first generation since Genesis with the power to threaten the created order. We cannot remain silent in the face of such danger. Why do we address these issues? We are simply trying to live up to the call of Jesus to be peacemakers in our own time and situation.

What are we saying? Fundamentally, we are saying that the decisions about nuclear weapons are among the most pressing moral questions of our age. While these decisions have obvious military and political aspects, they involve fundamental moral choices. In simple terms, we are saying that good ends (defending one's country, protecting freedom, etc.) cannot justify immoral means (the use of weapons which kill indiscriminately and threaten whole societies). We fear that our world and nation are headed in the wrong direction. More weapons with greater destructive potential are produced every day. More and more nations are seeking to become nuclear powers. In our quest for more and more security we fear we are actually becoming less and less secure.

In the words of our Holy Father, we need a "moral about-face." The whole world must summon the moral courage and technical means to say no to nuclear conflict; no to weapons of mass destruction; no to an arms race which robs the poor and the vulnerable; and no to the moral danger of a nuclear age which places before humankind indefensible choices of constant terror or surrender. Peacemaking is not an optional commitment. It is a requirement of our faith. We are called to be peacemakers, not by some movement of the moment, but by our Lord Jesus. The content and context of our peacemaking is set not by some political agenda or ideological program, but by the teaching of his Church.

Ultimately, this letter is intended as an expression of Christian faith, affirming the confidence we have that the risen Lord remains with us precisely in moments of crisis. It is our belief in his presence and power among us which sustains us in confronting the awesome challenge of the nuclear age. We speak from faith to provide hope for all who recognize the challenge and are working to confront it with the resources of faith and reason.

To approach the nuclear issue in faith is to recognize our absolute need for prayer: we urge and invite all to unceasing prayer for peace with justice for all people. In a spirit of prayerful hope we present this message of peace.

Excerpts from
"The Challenge of Peace:
God's Promise and Our Response"

National Conference of Catholic Bishops

Introduction

The crisis of which we speak arises from this fact: Nuclear war threatens the existence of our planet; this is a more menacing threat than any the world has known. It is neither tolerable nor necessary that human beings live under this threat. But removing it will require a major effort of intelligence, courage and faith. As Pope John Paul II said at Hiroshima: "From now on it is only through a conscious choice and through a deliberate policy that humanity can survive."

As Americans, citizens of the nation which was first to produce atomic weapons, which has been the only one to use them and which today is one of the handful of nations capable of decisively influencing the course of the nuclear age, we have grave human, moral and political responsibilities to see that a "conscious choice" is made to save humanity. This letter is therefore both an invitation and a challenge to Catholics in the United States to join with others in shaping the conscious choices and deliberate policies required in this "moment of supreme crisis."

The nuclear threat transcends religious, cultural and national boundaries. To confront its danger requires all the resources reason and faith can muster. This letter is a contribution to a wider common effort meant to call Catholics and all members of our political community to dialogue and specific decisions about this awesome question.

I. Peace in the Modern World: Religious Perspectives and Principles

The pastoral constitution on the Church in the Modern World of the Second Vatican Council calls us to bring the light of the Gospel to bear upon "the signs of the times." Three signs of the times have particularly influenced the writing of this letter. The first, to quote Pope John Paul II at the United Nations, is that "the world wants peace, the world needs peace." The second is the judgment of Vatican II about the arms race: "The arms race is one of the greatest curses on the human race and the harm it inflicts upon the poor is more than can be endured." The third is the way in which the unique dangers and dynamics of the nuclear arms race present qualitatively new problems which must be addressed by fresh applications of traditional moral principles. In light of these three characteristics, we wish to examine Catholic teaching on peace and war.

Building peace within and among nations is the work of many individuals and institutions; it is the fruit of ideas and decisions taken in the political, cultural, economic, social, military and legal sectors of life. We believe that the church, as a community of faith and social institution, has a proper, necessary and distinctive part to play in the pursuit of peace.

The distinctive contribution of the church flows from her religious nature and ministry. The church is called to be in a unique way the instrument of the kingdom of God in history. Since peace is one of the signs of that kingdom present in the world, the church fulfills part of her essential mission by making the peace of the kingdom more visible in our time.

A. Peace and the Kingdom

A theology of peace should ground the task of peacemaking solidly in the biblical vision of the kingdom of God, then place it centrally in the ministry of the church.

Ezekiel, who promised a covenant of peace, condemned in no uncertain terms the false prophets who said there was peace in the land while idolatry and injustice continued (Ezek. 13:16). Jeremiah followed in this tradition and berated those who "healed the wounds of the people lightly" and proclaimed peace while injustice and infidelity prevailed (Jer. 6:14; 8:10-12). Jeremiah and Isaiah both condemned the leaders when, against true security, they depended upon their own strength or alliances with other nations rather than trusting in God (Isa. 7:1-9; 30:1-4; Jer. 37:10). The lament of Isaiah 48:18 makes clear the connection between justice, fidelity to God's law and peace; he cries out: "O that you had hearkened to my commandments! Then your peace would have been like a river, and your righteousness like the waves of the sea."

The Old Testament provides us with the history of a people who portrayed their God as one who intervened in their lives, who protected them and led them to freedom, often as a mighty leader in battle. They also appear as a people who longed constantly for peace. Such peace was always seen as a result of God's gift which came about in fidelity to the covenantal union. Furthermore, in the midst of their unfulfilled longing, God's people clung tenaciously to hope in the promise of an eschatological time when, in the fullness of salvation, peace and justice would embrace and all creation would be secure from harm. The people looked for a Messiah, one whose coming would signal the beginning of that time. In their waiting, they heard the prophets call them to love according to the covenantal vision, to repent and to be ready for God's reign.

Jesus proclaimed the reign of God in his words and made it present in his actions. His words begin with a call to conversion and a proclamation of the arrival of the kingdom. "The time is fulfilled, and the kingdom of God is at hand; repent, and believe in the gospel" (Mark 1:15; Matt. 4:17). The call to conversion was at the same time an invitation to enter God's reign. Jesus went beyond the prophets' cries for conversion when he declared that, in him, the reign of God had begun and was in fact among the people (Luke 17:20-21; 12:32).

The words of Jesus would remain an impossible, abstract ideal were it not for two things: the actions of Jesus and his gift of the Spirit. In his actions Jesus showed the way of living in God's reign; he manifested the forgiveness which he called for when he accepted all who came to him, forgave their sins, healed them, released them from the demons who possessed them. In doing these things he made the tender mercy of God present in a world which knew violence, oppression and injustice. Jesus pointed out the injustices of his time and opposed those who laid burdens upon the people or defiled true worship.

Jesus refused to defend himself with force or with violence. He endured violence and cruelty so that God's love might be fully manifest and the world might be reconciled to the One from whom it had become estranged. Even at his death Jesus cried out for forgiveness for those who were his executioners: "Father, forgive them" (Luke 23:34).

The resurrection of Jesus is the sign to the world that God indeed does reign, does give life in death and that the love of God is stronger even than death (Rom. 8:36-39).

Only in light of this, the fullest demonstration of the power of God's reign, can Jesus' gift of peace—a peace which the world cannot give (John 14:27)—be understood.

Because we have been gifted with God's peace in the risen Christ, we are called to our own peace and to the making of peace in our world. As disciples and as children of God it is our task to seek for ways in which to make the forgiveness, justice and mercy, and love of God visible in a world where violence and enmity are too often the norm. When we listen to God's word, we hear again and always the call to repentance and to belief: to repentance because, although we are redeemed we continue to need redemption; to belief because although the reign of God is near, it is still seeking its fullness.

B. Kingdom and History

Christian hope about history is rooted in our belief in God as creator and sustainer of our existence and our conviction that the kingdom of God will come in spite of sin, human weakness and failure. It is precisely because sin is part of history that the realization of the peace of the kingdom is never permanent or total.

Christians are called to live the tension between the vision of the reign of God and its concrete realization in history. The tension is often described in terms of "already but not yet": i.e., we already live in the grace of the kingdom, but it is not yet the completed kingdom. Hence, we are a pilgrim people in a world marked by conflict and injustice. Christ's grace is at work in the world; his command of love and his call to reconciliation are not purely future ideals but call us to obedience today.

This recognition—that peace is possible but never assured and that its possibility must be continually protected and preserved in the face of obstacles and attacks upon it—accounts in large measure for the complexity of Catholic teaching on warfare. In the kingdom of God peace and justice will be fully realized. Justice is always the foundation of peace. In history, efforts to pursue both peace and justice are at times in tension, and the struggle for justice may threaten certain forms of peace.

C. The Moral Choices for the Kingdom

In one of its most frequently quoted passages the pastoral constitution declared that it is necessary "to undertake a completely fresh reappraisal of war." The council's teaching situates this call for a "fresh reappraisal" within the context of a broad analysis of the dignity of the human person and the state of the world today. If we lose sight of this broader discussion we cannot grasp the council's wisdom. For the issue of war and peace confronts everyone with a basic question: What contributes to and what impedes the construction of a more genuinely human world? If we are to evaluate war with an entirely new attitude, we must be serious about approaching the human person with an entirely new attitude. The obligation for all of humanity to work toward universal respect for human rights and human dignity is a fundamental imperative of the social, economic and political order.

1. The Nature of Peace

The Catholic tradition has always understood the meaning of peace in positive terms. Peace is both a gift of God and a human work. It must be constructed on the basis of central human values: truth, justice, freedom and love. The pastoral constitution states the traditional conception of peace:

> Peace is not merely the absence of war. Nor can it be reduced solely to the maintenance of a balance of power between enemies. Nor is it brought about by dictatorship. Instead, it is rightly and appropriately called "an enterprise of justice" (Isa. 32:7). Peace results from that harmony built into human society by its divine founder and actualized by men as they thirst after ever greater justice.

2. The Presumption Against War and the Principle of Legitimate Self-Defense

Under the rubric "curbing the savagery of war," the council contemplates the "melancholy state of humanity." It looks at this world as it is, not simply as we would want it to be. The view is stark: ferocious new means of warfare threatening savagery surpassing that of the past, deceit, subversion, terrorism, genocide. This last crime in particular is vehemently condemned as horrendous, but all activities which deliberately conflict with the all-embracing principles of universal natural law, which is permanently binding, are criminal, as are all orders commanding such action. Supreme commendation is due the courage

of those who openly and fearlessly resist those who issue such commands.

The Christian has no choice but to defend peace, properly understood, against aggression. This is an inalienable obligation. It is the *how*
of defending peace which offers moral options. We stress this principle
again because we observe so much misunderstanding about both those
who resist bearing arms and those who bear them. Great numbers from
both traditions provide examples of exceptional courage, examples the
world continues to need.

Catholic teaching sees these two distinct moral responses as
having a complementary relationship in the sense that both seek to
serve the common good. They differ in their perception of how the common good is to be defended most effectively, but both responses testify
to the Christian conviction that peace must be pursued and rights
defended within moral restraints and in the context of defining other
basic human values.

We believe work to develop non-violent means of fending off aggression and resolving conflict best reflects the call of Jesus both to love
and to justice. Indeed, each increase in the potential destructiveness of
weapons and therefore of war serves to underline the rightness of the
way that Jesus mandated to his followers. But, on the other hand, the
fact of aggression, oppression and injustice in our world also serves to
legitimate the resort to weapons and armed force in defense of justice.
We must recognize the reality of the paradox we face as Christians living in the context of the world as it presently exists; we must continue
to articulate our belief that love is possible and the only real hope for
all human relations, and yet accept that force, even deadly force, is
sometimes justified and that nations must provide for their defense. It
is the mandate of Christians in the face of this paradox to strive to re-
solve it through an even greater commitment to Christ and his message.

3. The Just-War Criteria

The moral theory of the "just-war" or "limited-war" doctrine begins
with the presumption which binds all Christians: We should do no harm
to our neighbors; how we treat our enemy is the key test of whether we
love our neighbor; and the possibility of taking even one human life is
a prospect we should consider in fear and trembling. How is it possible
to move from these presumptions to the idea of a justifiable use of lethal
force?

Just-war teaching has evolved . . . as an effort to prevent war; only if war cannot be rationally avoided does the teaching then seek to restrict and reduce its horrors. It does this by establishing a set of rigorous conditions which must be met if the decision to go to war is to be morally permissible. Such a decision, especially today, requires extraordinarily strong reasons for overriding the presumption *in favor of peace* and *against* war. This is one significant reason why valid just-war teaching makes provision for conscientious dissent. It is presumed that all sane people prefer peace, never *want* to initiate war and accept even the most justifiable defensive war only as a sad necessity. Only the most powerful reasons may be permitted to override such objection.

The determination of *when* conditions exist which allow the resort to force in spite of the strong presumption against it is made in light of *jus ad bellum* criteria. The determination of *how* even a justified resort to force must be conducted is made in light of the *jus in bello* criteria. We shall briefly explore the meaning of both.

Jus ad Bellum: Why and when recourse to war is permissible.

a. Just Cause

War is permissible only to confront "a real and certain danger," i.e., to protect innocent life, to preserve conditions necessary for decent human existence and to secure basic human rights. As both Pope Pius XII and Pope John XXIII made clear, if war of retribution was ever justifiable, the risks of modern war negate such a claim today.

b. Competent Authority

In the Catholic tradition the right to use force has always been joined to the common good; war must be declared by those with responsibility for public order, not by private groups or individuals.

While the legitimacy of revolution in some circumstances cannot be denied, just-war teachings must be applied as rigorously to revolutionary-counterrevolutionary conflicts as to others. The issue of who constitutes competent authority and how such authority is exercised is essential.

c. Comparative Justice

The category of comparative justice is designed to emphasize the presumption against war which stands at the beginning of just-war teaching. In a world of sovereign states recognizing neither a common moral authority nor a central political authority comparative justice stresses that no state should act on the basis that it has "absolute justice" on its side. Every party to a conflict should acknowledge the limits of its "just cause" and the consequent requirement to use *only* limited means in pursuit of its objectives.

d. Right Intention

Right intention is related to just cause—war can be legitimately intended only for the reasons set forth above as a just cause. During the conflict, right intention means pursuit of peace and reconciliation, including avoiding unnecessarily destructive acts or imposing unreasonable conditons (e.g., unconditional surrender).

e. Last Resort

For resort to war to be justified, all peaceful alternatives must have been exhausted.

f. Probability of Success

This is a difficult criterion to apply, but its purpose is to prevent irrational resort to force or hopeless resistance when the outcome of either will clearly be disproportionate or futile. The determination includes a recognition that at times defense of key values, even against great odds, may be a "proportionate" witness.

g. Proportionality

In terms of the *jus ad bellum* criteria, proportionality means that the damage to be inflicted and the costs incurred by war must be proportionate to the good expected by taking up arms. Nor should judgments concerning proportionality be limited to the temporal order without regard to a spiritual dimension in terms of "damage," "cost" and "the good expected." In today's interdependent world even a local conflict can affect people everywhere; this is particularly the case when the nuclear powers are involved. Hence a nation cannot justly go to war today without considering the effect of its action on others and on the international community.

Jus in Bello. Even when the stringent conditions which justify resort to war are met, the conduct of war (i.e., strategy, tactics and individual actions) remains subject to continuous scrutiny in light of two principles which have special significance today precisely because of the destructive capability of modern technological warfare. These principles are proportionality and discrimination. In discussing them here we shall apply them to the question of *jus ad bellum* as well as *jus in bello;* for today it becomes increasingly difficult to make a decision to use any kind of armed force, however limited initially in intention and in the destructive power of the weapons employed, without facing at least the possibility of escalation to broader, or even total, war and to the use of weapons of horrendous destructive potential.

The Pontifical Academy of Sciences in its November 1981 "Statement of the Consequences of Nuclear War" [stated]:

> Throughout its history humanity has been confronted with war, but since 1945 the nature of warfare has changed so profoundly that the future of the human race, of generations yet unborn, is imperiled. . . . For the first time it is possible to cause damage on such a catastrophic scale as to wipe out a large part of civilization and to endanger its very survival. The large-scale use of such weapons could trigger major and irreversible ecological and genetic changes whose limits cannot be predicted.

Response to aggression must not exceed the nature of the aggression. To destroy civilization as we know it by waging a "total war" as today it *could* be waged would be a monstrously disproportionate response to aggression on the part of any nation.

In terms of the arms race, if the *real* end in view is legitimate defense against unjust aggression and the means to this end are not evil in themselves, we must still examine the question of proportionality concerning attendant evils. Do the exorbitant costs, the general climate of insecurity generated, the possibility of accidental detonation of highly destructive weapons, the danger of error and miscalculation that could provoke retaliation and war—do such evils of others attendant upon and indirectly deriving from the arms race make the arms race itself a disproportionate response to aggression?

4. The Value of Non-Violence

Moved by the example of Jesus' life and by his teaching, some Christians have from the earliest days of the church committed themselves to a non-violent lifestyle.

The vision of Christian non-violence is not passive about injustice and the defense of the rights of others; it rather affirms and exemplifies what it means to resist injustice through non-violent methods.

In the development of a theology of peace and the growth of the Christian pacifist position among Catholics, these words of the pastoral constitution have special significance: "All these factors force us to undertake a completely fresh reappraisal of war." The council fathers had reference to "the development of armaments by modern science [which] has immeasurably magnified the horrors and wickedness of war." While the just-war teaching has clearly been in possession for the past 1,500 years of Catholic thought, the "new moment" in which we find ourselves sees the just-war teaching and non-violence as distinct but interdependent methods of evaluating warfare. They diverge on some specific conclusions, but they share a common presumption against the use of force as a means of settling disputes.

Both find their roots in the Christian theological tradition; each contributes to the full moral vision we need in pursuit of a human peace. We believe the two perspectives support and complement one another, each preserving the other from distortion. Finally, in an age of technological warfare, analysis from the viewpoint of non-violence and analysis from the viewpoint of the just-war teaching often converge and agree in their opposition to methods of warfare which are in fact indistinguishable from total warfare.

II. War and Peace in the Modern World: Problems and Principles

Both the just-war teaching and non-violence are confronted with a unique challenge by nuclear warfare.

In the nuclear arsenals of the United States or the Soviet Union alone there exists a capacity to do something no other age could imagine: We can threaten the entire planet. For people of faith this means we read the Book of Genesis with a new awareness; the moral issue at stake in nuclear war involves the meaning of sin in its most graphic dimensions. Every sinful act is a confrontation of the creature and the Creator. Today the destructive potential of the nuclear powers threatens the human person, the civilization we have slowly constructed and even the created order itself.

We live today, therefore, in the midst of a cosmic drama; we possess a power which should never be used, but which might be used if we do not reverse our direction. We live with nuclear weapons knowing we cannot afford to make one serious mistake. This fact dramatizes the precariousness of our position, politically, morally and spiritually.

Traditionally the church's moral teaching sought first to prevent war and then to limit its consequences if it occurred. Today the possibilities for placing political and moral limits on nuclear war are so minimal that the moral task, like the medical, is prevention: As a people, we must refuse to legitimate the idea of nuclear war. Such a refusal will require not only new ideas and new vision, but what the Gospel calls conversion of the heart.

We see with increasing clarity the political folly of a system which threatens mutual suicide, the psychological damage this does to ordinary people, especially the young, the economic distortion of priorities—billions readily spent for destructive instruments while pitched battles are waged daily in our legislatures over much smaller amounts for the homeless, the hungry and the helpless here and abroad. But it is much less clear how we translate a no to nuclear war into the personal and public choices which can move us in a new direction, toward a national policy and an international system which more adequately reflect the values and vision of the kingdom of God.

III. The Arms Race and Economic Development

It is in the context of the United Nations that the impact of the arms race on the prospects for economic development is highlighted. The numerous U.N. studies on the relationship of development and disarmament support the judgment of Vatican II cited earlier in this letter: "The arms race is one of the greatest curses on the human race and the harm it inflicts upon the poor is more than can be endured."

We are aware that the precise relationship between disarmament and development is neither easily demonstrated nor easily reoriented. But the fact of a massive distortion of resources in the face of crying human need creates a moral question. In an interdependent world the security of one nation is related to the security of all. When we consider how and what we pay for defense today, we need a broader view than the equation of arms with security. The threats to the security and stability of an interdependent world are not all contained in missiles and bombers.

An interdependent world requires an understanding that key policy questions today involve mutuality of interest. If the monetary and trading systems are not governed by sensitivity to mutual needs, they can be destroyed. If the protection of human rights and the promotion of human needs are left as orphans in the diplomatic arena, the stability we seek in increased armaments will eventually be threatened by rights denied and needs unmet in vast sectors of the globe. If future planning about conservation of and access to resources is relegated to a pure struggle of power, we shall simply guarantee conflict in the future.

IV. The Pastoral Challenge and Response

We recommend and endorse for the faithful some practical programs to meet the challenge to their faith in this area of grave concern.

1. Educational Programs and Formation of Conscience

Since war, especially the threat of nuclear war, is one of the central problems of our day, how we seek to solve it could determine the mode and even the possibility of life on earth. God made human beings stewards of the earth; we cannot escape this responsibility. Therefore we urge every diocese and parish to implement balanced and objective educational programs to help people at all age levels to understand better the issues of war and peace. Development and implementation of such programs must receive a high priority during the next several years.

2. True Peace Calls for "Reverence for Life"

All of the values we are promoting in this letter rest ultimately in the disarmament of the human heart and the conversion of the human spirit to God, who alone can give authentic peace. Indeed, to have peace in our world we must first have peace within ourselves. Interior peace becomes possible only when we have a conversion of spirit. We cannot have peace with hate in our hearts.

No society can live in peace with itself or with the world without a full awareness of the worth and dignity of every human person and of the sacredness of all human life (James 4:1-2). When we accept violence in any form as commonplace, our sensitivities become dulled. When we accept violence, war itself can be taken for granted. Violence has many faces: oppression of the poor, deprivation of basic human rights, economic exploitation, sexual exploitation and pornography, neglect or abuse of the aged and the helpless and innumerable other acts of inhumanity. Abortion in particular blunts a sense of the sacredness of human life. In a society where the innocent unborn are killed wantonly, how can we expect people to feel righteous revulsion at the act or threat of killing non-combatants in war?

3. Prayer

A conversion of our hearts and minds will make it possible for us to enter into a closer communion with our Lord. We nourish that communion by personal and communal prayer, for it is in prayer that we encounter Jesus, who is our peace and learn from him the way to peace.

We implore other Christians and everyone of good will to join us in this continuing prayer for peace, as we beseech God for peace within ourselves, in our families and community, in our nation and in the world.

4. Penance

Prayer by itself is incomplete without penance. Penance directs us toward our goal of putting on the attitudes of Jesus himself. Because we are all capable of violence, we are never totally conformed to Christ and are always in need of conversion. The 20th century alone provides adequate evidence of our violence as individuals and as a nation. Thus, there is continual need for acts of penance and conversion. The worship of the church, particularly through the sacrament of reconciliation and communal penance services, offers us multiple ways to make reparation for the violence in our own world.

As a tangible sign of our need and desire to do penance we, for the cause of peace, commit ourselves to fast and abstinence on each Friday of the year. We call upon our people voluntarily to do penance on Friday by eating less food and by abstaining from meat. This return to a traditional practice of penance, once well observed in the U.S. church, should be accompanied by works of charity and service toward our neighbors. Every Friday should be a day significantly devoted to prayer, penance and almsgiving for peace.

V. Challenge and Hope

The arms race presents questions of conscience we may not evade. As American Catholics we are called to express our loyalty to the deepest values we cherish: peace, justice and security for the entire human family. National goals and policies must be measured against that standard.

We speak here in a specific way to the Catholic community. After the passage of nearly four decades and a concomitant growth in our understanding of the ever growing horror of nuclear war, we must shape the climate of opinion which will make it possible for our country to express profound sorrow over the atomic bombing in 1945. Without that sorrow, there is no possibility of finding a way to repudiate future use of nuclear weapons or of conventional weapons in such military actions as would not fulfill just-war criteria.

To Educators: We have outlined in this letter Catholic teaching on war and peace, but this framework will become a living message only through your work in the Catholic community. To teach the ways of peace is not "to weaken the nation's will," but to be concerned for the nation's soul. We address theologians in a particular way because we know that we have only begun the journey toward a theology of peace.

To Parents: Your role, in our eyes, is unsurpassed by any other; the foundation of society is the family. We are conscious of the continuing sacrifices you make in the efforts to nurture the full human and spiritual growth of your children. Children hear the gospel message first from your lips. Parents who consciously discuss issues of justice in the home and who strive to help children solve conflicts through non-violent methods enable their children to grow up as peacemakers. We pledge our continuing pastoral support in the common objective we share of building a peaceful world for the future of children everywhere.

To Youth: Pope John Paul II singles you out in every country where he visits as the hope of the future; we agree with him. We call you to choose your future work and professions carefully. How you spend the rest of your lives will determine in large part whether there will any longer be a world as we know it. We ask you to study carefully the teachings of the church and the demands of the Gospel about war and peace. We encourage you to seek careful guidance as you reach conscientious decisions about your civic responsibilities in this age of nuclear military forces.

To Men and Women in Military Service: We remind all in authority and in the chain of command that their training and field manuals have long prohibited, and still do prohibit, certain actions in the conduct of war, especially those actions which inflict harm of innocent civilians. The question is not whether certain measures are unlawful or forbidden in warfare, but which measures: To refuse to take such actions is not an act of cowardice or treason but one of courage and patriotism.

Those who train individuals for military duties must remember that the citizen does not lose his or her basic human rights by entrance into military service. No one, for whatever reason, can justly treat a military person with less dignity and respect than that demanded for and deserved by every human person. One of the most difficult problems of war involves defending a free society without destroying the values that give it meaning and validity.

To Men and Women in Defense Industries: You also face specific questions because the defense industry is directly involved in the development and production of the weapons of mass destruction which have concerned us in this letter. We do not presume or pretend that clear answers exist to many of the personal, professional and financial choices facing you in your varying responsibilities. In this letter we have ruled out certain uses of nuclear weapons, while also expressing conditional moral acceptance for deterrence. All Catholics, at every level of defense industries, can and should use the moral principles of this letter to form their consciences.

To Men and Women of Science: Modern history is not lacking scientists who have looked back with deep remorse on the development of weapons to which they contributed, sometimes with the highest motivation, even believing that they were creating weapons that would render all other weapons obsolete and convince the world of the unthinkableness of war. Such efforts have ever proved illusory. Surely equivalent dedication of scientific minds to reverse current trends and to pursue concepts as bold and adventuresome in favor of peace as those which in the past have magnified the risks of war could result in dramatic benefits for all of humanity.

To Public Officials: Leadership in a nuclear world means examining with great care and objectivity every potential initiative toward world peace, regardless of how unpromising it might at first appear. One specific initiative which might be taken now would be the establishment of a task force including the public sector, industry, labor, economists and scientists with the mandate to consider nuclear disarmament to our economic well-being and industrial output.

To Catholics as Citizens: In the wider public discussion we look forward in a special way to cooperating with all other Christians with whom we share the same common traditions. We also treasure cooperative efforts with Jewish and Islamic communities, which possess a long and abiding concern for peace as a religious and human value. Finally, we reaffirm our desire to participate in a common public effort with all men and women of good will who seek to reverse the arms race and secure the peace of the world.

Peacemaking: The Believers' Calling

Presbyterian Church (USA)

Call to Peacemaking—An Affirmation of Policy and Direction

Twenty centuries ago, "in the fullness of time," God sent Jesus the Christ. Now there is a special time in history—a season *(kairos)*—summoning the faith and obedience of God's people. For Christ has gathered and deployed his people around the earth, across political and economic lines, in places of powerfully protected affluence, and among the poorest of the poor. The body of Christ responds to the world's pain with empathy and anguish, one part for another, in our time.

Ominous clouds hang over human history. There are frightening risks in the continuing arms race and looming conflicts over diminishing energy resources as centers of power struggle for control. Our fear for safety has led us to trust in the false security of arms; our sin of war has led us to take life; and now we are in danger of taking our own lives as well. Furthermore, economic systems fail to allow a quarter of the world's population full participation in their societies, creating recurrent patterns of starvation and famine in Asia and Africa as in the 1970s.

But we believe that these times, so full of peril and tragedy for the human family, present a special call for obedience to our Lord, the Prince of Peace. The Spirit is calling us to life out of death.

The church must discern the signs of the times in the light of what the Spirit is revealing. We see signs of resurrection as the Spirit moves the churches to call for peace. We are at a turning point. We are faced with the decision either to serve the Rule of God or to side with the powers of death through our complacency and silence.

In these days we know that Jesus was sent by God into all the world. As we break bread together, our eyes are opened and we recognize his living presence among us—Christ crucified by the tragic inequities on the earth—calling us together.

We are Christ's people, compelled by the Spirit and guided by our creeds to listen to a gospel that is addressed to the whole world. We are gathered around the Lord's Table with people from North and South and East and West. A new integrity is required of us: integrity in worship, integrity in secular life, integrity in relationship with Christ and Christians everywhere.

There is a new sense of the oneness of the world in our time. Humankind's initial forays into space have created a new perspective, a dramatic sense of the earth—the whole earth—as home. The era of satellite communication systems and the migration of millions of people from continent to continent have produced a new awareness of conditions of life everywhere on the globe.

It is not possible, in such a time, to avoid awareness of the economic disparities and political oppression besetting the human family. It is not possible to escape the knowledge of human suffering, and it is not possible to ignore the incongruous juxtaposition of affluence and arms on the one hand, and poverty and oppression on the other. The futility of nuclear war on a small planet as a solution to human problems is apparent.

We know that there can be no national security without global security and no global security without political and economic justice. As God's people, we will not cry "Peace, peace" without the fullness of God's shalom. As God's people, we will seek the security of the whole human family—all for whom Christ died. As God's people, we will celebrate the dignity of each of God's children.

We know that peace cannot be achieved simply by ending the arms race unless there is economic and political justice in the human family. Peace is more than the absence of war, more than a precarious balance of powers. Peace is the intended order of the world with life abundant for all God's children. Peacemaking is the calling of the Christian church, for Christ is our peace who has made us one through his body on the cross.

How will peace be achieved? By disarmament? Certainly, but not only by disarmament. By global economic reform? Certainly, but not only by global economic reform. By the change of political structures? Basically, at the heart, it is a matter of the way we see the world through the eyes of Christ. It is a matter of praying and yearning. It is an inner response to God, who loves the whole world and whose Spirit calls for and empowers the making of peace.

With repentance and humility and the power of hope, let us tend to our task.

To that end the 192nd General Assembly (1980) affirms peacemaking as the responsibility of the United Presbyterian Church and declares:

1. *The church is faithful to Christ when it is engaged in peacemaking.* God wills shalom—justice and peace on earth. "Blessed are the peacemakers, for they shall be called children of God," said our Lord, the Prince of Peace. Those who follow our Lord have a special calling as peacemakers. In our confessions of faith the church has recognized this vocation, yet in our life we have been unfaithful to our Lord. We must repent. Our insensitivity to today's patterns of injustice, inequality, and oppression—indeed, our participation in them—denies the gospel. Christ alone is our peace. As part of his body in the whole church, we experience the brokenness of this world in our own life. Today we stand at a turning point in history. Our structures of military might, economic relations, political institutions, and cultural patterns fail to meet the needs of our time. At stake is our future and our integrity as God's people.

2. *The church is obedient to Christ when it nurtures and equips God's people as peacemakers.* The church expects the gifts and guidance of the Holy Spirit in this task (Eph. 4:1- 16). Where the church is obedient to Christ, congregations will come alive in peacemaking. In worship we recognize the presence of God with us in our poor fragile lives. We live by the faith that God alone has cosmic dominion, that Christ alone is the Lord of the church and history, that the Holy Spirit alone empowers us here and now. We realize afresh that we are engaged in spiritual struggle.

In the proclamation of God's word of judgment and promise we are freed from guilt and paralyzing fear; at the Lord's Table we discover our brothers and sisters around the world; in baptism we are united in solidarity with the whole body; in prayer we lift our concern for the victims of injustice, oppression, and warfare; in praise we celebrate the gift of life, the Prince of Peace; in study we focus on foreign policy subjects in light of biblical and theological considerations.

The General Assembly has established positions on many subjects related to peace and justice, providing directions to facilitate the study and action necessary to equip God's people for the ordering of the church's life and the establishment of public policies in support of peacemaking. . . . The report on "Peacemaking: The Believers' Calling" is a logical and even essential place to start in study and equipment for witnessing. Interaction at the congregational level on the issues discussed in that report and in past actions of the General Assembly raises consciousness and transforms sensitivities about other peoples and their needs, about justice, and about the directions of United States foreign policy. Contact with other members of the worldwide Christian community enhances our growth as peacemakers.

Through worship and study we are miraculously strengthened by God's grace, and find new energy for action and a new sense of vocation crucial to peacemaking and the buoyant Christian life.

3. *The church bears witness to Christ when it nourishes the moral life of the nation for the sake of peace in our world.* The church's faithful obedience to its calling means active participation in the formation of the values and beliefs of our society. It means seeking peace in the personal and social relationships of our culture and exercising our citizenship in the body politic to shape foreign policy. It is of strategic importance for us to nurture changes in public attitude and to raise public consciousness.

By God's grace we are members of a world community and can bring our global insights and peacemaking to our particular settings. By God's grace we are freed to work with all people who strive for peace and justice and to serve as signposts for God's love in our broken world. To deny our calling is a disservice to the church and the world. To affirm our calling is to act in "faith, hope and love." The love of Christ constrains us. The choices may be difficult, but there is no substitute for acting as a church on the specific foreign policy problems affecting peace in our world today. Our "strength is in [our] confidence that God's purpose rather than [human] schemes will finally prevail" (Confession of 1967 [9.25]).

In such assurance all United Presbyterians are challenged to worship, study, and live boldly in Christ, as expressed in this Psalm of Peacemaking:

A Psalm of Peacemaking

We live in a time of *kairos*
when humanity stands on the border of a promised time,

when God's people are summoned to obedience and faithfulness
    to preserve God's creation,
    to stand with the poor and oppressed everywhere, and
    to stand together as the people of the earth;
when with confession and with humility we repent of
    our blindness to the division and war in our own hearts and in
        our own land,
    our obsession with money and our pursuit of power,
    our irrational belief in security through weaponry, and
    our worship of secular gods.
We are called
    to be obedient to Jesus Christ, the Prince of Peace,
        who loves the whole world and
        who invites us to be stewards of the earth and servants of his
            people,
    to be co-workers in the new Creation.
Let us be peacemakers.
Let us be called the children of God,
    speaking boldly with moral conviction to the nation and to the world,
    building, with God's grace, a new moral order in the world
        community; and
    acting now for world peace, an enterprise of justice,
        an outcome of love.

Congregational "Commitment to Peacemaking"

Presbyterian Church (USA)

Through Christ Jesus, the world is reconciled to God, and all humanity is offered God's peace. God's peace (shalom) overcomes brokenness and despair and offers us the possibility of wholeness and peace in our own lives, our families, communities, and in the international arena.

Why does the church do peacemaking? Peacemaking is a priority of the church because we are a people who have experienced God's peace. We do peacemaking because God has given to the church the ministry of reconciliation.

The 195th General Assembly (1983) urged the sessions of each congregation in the Presbyterian Church (USA) to consider making a commitment to integrate peacemaking into the life and mission of the congregation. The "Commitment to Peacemaking," which was commended by the General Assembly, is one way that a commitment might be expressed. Each session is urged to seriously consider making such a commitment.

God's Covenant with creation is given as grace and peace. Peace (shalom) is the wholeness and community in which human beings are meant to live. Although all people are sinners, God continually renews the Covenant through our Lord Jesus Christ. God's peace heals, comforts, strengthens, and frees.

Responding to this good news, the church goes into the whole world to point to and become a part of God's peacegiving. God's peace is offered wherever there is brokenness—in individual lives, families, congregations, communities and nations. In God's Covenant, the world and the church experience wholeness, security and justice.

The 1983 General Assembly has affirmed in "Peacemaking: The Believers' Calling" that God's peacegiving in a broken and insecure world is central to the message of the gospel. Therefore people of faith engage in peacemaking, not as a peripheral activity, but as an integral part of their congregational life and mission.

Responding to God's Covenant, the session of the _____
_____ Church now commits itself to
peacemaking during this decade. In fulfilling this commitment, we will:

help to provide worship that points to the reality of God's peacegiving;

encourage the members of the congregation to receive God's peace in
their own lives and, through prayer and Bible study, to seek it for
today's world;

enable and equip members of the congregation to grow as peacemakers
in their families, in the congregation and in the community;

help the congregation to work for social, racial and economic justice,
and respond to people in the community who are caught in poverty,
hurt by unemployment, or burdened by other problems;

encourage the congregation to support human rights and economic justice efforts in at least one area of the world, such as Central America,
southern Africa, the Middle East, East Asia, East Europe, or Central
Asia;

work to end the arms race, to reverse the worldwide growth of militarism, and to reduce tension among nations;

support financially the churchwide peacemaking effort, through the
Special Peacemaking Offering on World Communion Sunday, the
Presbyterian Peacemaking Fund, or other means.

The session will lead and support the congregation in this
peacemaking response to God's Covenant. We will appoint a member
or committee to be our contact with the presbytery peacemaking task
force and with the Presbyterian Peacemaking Program to receive and
distribute information and resource materials which will help us to fulfill this commitment.

Signed _____
                        Moderator of Session   *Date*

Signed _____
                        Clerk of Session   *Date*

(You might wish to retain this signed page for your records.)

Christian Faith and the Nuclear Arms Race: A Reformed Perspective

Reformed Church in America

Introduction

God is the ultimate subject of theological reflection. The nuclear arms race may well be regarded as the penultimate subject for our time. There is no greater affront to the Lord and Giver of life, no more convincing evidence of human enslavement to the dark powers of this age, and no more urgent cause for the church's prophetic witness and action.

In 1959 Karl Barth decried "the blasphemous, deadly development of atomic weapons" and the church's failure to oppose them.[1] In the early 1960s Helmut Gollwitzer declared: "The church must speak out clearly against atomic war. . . . This No to atomic war has not been arbitrarily arrived at by the church but is a command given to it by God."[2] More recently, condemnations of nuclear weapons and calls to disarmament have issued from many and diverse quarters within the church including the National Council of Churches, the Southern Baptist Convention, the National Conference of Catholic Bishops, the United Presbyterian Church, U.S.A., and the Presbyterian Church in the United States (Southern), Billy Graham, and Pope John Paul II. This emerging consensus is overdue, for the world is on the brink of another and more terrible escalation in the nuclear arms race.

The General Synod of 1979 accepted eight specific recommendations which constituted a "Call to Action" concerning the nuclear arms race and disarmament (*MGS,* 1979, pp. 95-97). We note especially the second and sixth of those recommendations:

> to call for a full and general prohibition of: nuclear arms testing; development and deployment of new nuclear weapon systems; production

A Report from the Theological Commission, General Synod 1980

and accumulation of chemical and radiological arms as well as other weapons of mass destruction.

to urge our churches in their teaching and preaching programs to emphasize the biblical vision of peace and to stress the devastating social and personal consequences of the arms race.

The Theological Commission submits this study to assist the church in acting upon the above recommendations and to offer a Reformed theological perspective on the nuclear arms race and the disarmament challenge.

The War That Cannot Be Won

Since the dawn of the nuclear era, people have noted with varying degrees of alarm that the human race has acquired the means for its own destruction. These means have been expanded to overkill proportions during this 35-year period, despite much talk about disarmament and several weak treaties. The United States, with its strategic triad of land-based intercontinental ballistic missiles (ICBMs), submarine-launched ballistic missiles, and strategic bombers, is now able to launch at least 8,500 independently targetable nuclear warheads. The Soviet Union armed with a similar triad is thought capable of delivering about 4,000 nuclear warheads.[3] The U.S. has been the leader in strategic nuclear technology from the beginning. Recently, however, advances by the Soviet Union have caused U.S. Secretary of Defense Harold Brown to assert that the two superpowers have now reached a point of "essential equivalence" in nuclear weapons capability. This language is deceptively simple, for both nations possess and continue to amass weapons stockpiles far in excess of any conceivable use or threat. The Pentagon has estimated that a mere one hundred nuclear warheads descending on the Soviet Union would pose a sufficient deterrent threat, destroying a minimum of 37 million people and 59 percent of that nation's industrial capacity. While the need for 8,500 existing warheads defies all logic, the U.S. continues to add to its stockpile at a rate of 3 per day.[4] This nuclear force of 8,000 megatons (equivalent to 8,000 million tons of TNT) represents a destructive capability equal to 615,000 Hiroshima atom bombs and is sufficient to destroy the world's population 12 times over. The Soviet Union and other nuclear armed nations possess an additional 8,000 megatons.

The quantitative dimensions of the nuclear arms race are awesome indeed and sufficient mandate for disarmament. They are not, however, the gravest aspect of the problem. Qualitative improvements in nuclear weapons technology will render the future far more dangerous than the present or the past. The new U.S. Trident, Cruise, and MX missiles, for example, represent significant qualitative advances in strategic capability, thus posing grave threats to the existing balance of power. Their deadly accuracy and immunity to detection and verification are certain to create intense anxiety to the Soviet Union, impede further arms limitation agreements, and escalate the arms race as the Russians seek to protect themselves by developing comparable weapons.

The present situation of "essential equivalence" offers the superpowers a rare, historic opportunity. From this point of parity, they could agree to a process of multilateral disarmament rather than launching another escalation in their vain quest for strategic superiority. Resistance to the SALT II treaty in the U.S. Senate, recent increases in U.S. military spending, NATO acceptance of new cruise and Pershing missiles in Europe, and the Soviet invasion of Afghanistan are woeful evidence that this opportunity will not be seized. Experts are predicting instead a new generation of weapons systems far exceeding present destructive potential; highly accurate guidance systems and warheads, computer equipment for limited nuclear war, new and more powerful ICBMs, lasers, and killer satellites.[5]

Particularly ominous is the shift which these new technologies make possible from a defensive strategy of deterrence to an offensive, "first strike," or "counterforce" strategy. Attempts are underway to make limited nuclear war an acceptable instrument of foreign policy.[6] The current administration in Washington has stated (as have the previous two) that the United States regards a first use of nuclear weapons to be one option for the protection of its vital interests. As recently as February 1980, a Pentagon study raised this specter with regard to a U.S. defense of the Persian Gulf area. In light of recent developments, the defensive strategies of previous decades seem almost benign compared to the insidious technologies and aggressive policies that threaten the future.

Even if nuclear war between the superpowers can be avoided, the nuclear arms race will continue to impoverish and imperil life on this planet. The health hazards of the nuclear era, for example, are enormous. Radiation in sufficient doses kills instantly. Where exposure is far more limited, it causes cancers. As lethal nuclear wastes accumulate in growing quantities, their carcinogenic and mutagenic properties jeopardize the ecosphere, the food chain, and the very genetic structure of the human species. The economic impact of the arms race is devastating. Excessive military expenditures fuel inflation, create unemployment, and consume vast sums that could be used to alleviate human suffering, respond to pressing social needs, and reduce taxes.

As the circle of nuclear armed nations grows, so does the grave risk of a regional nuclear conflict that could quickly engulf the super powers. Largely due to the exportation of nuclear power plants, 35 nations will have the material to produce nuclear weapons within the next decade. (Pakistan recently announced its imminent deployment of "an Islamic atom bomb.")[7] This proliferation increases the probability that nuclear weapons will fall into the hands of unstable governments or terrorist groups. Not to be overlooked are the very real possibilities that nuclear war may be triggered by computer malfunction or human error. At least five such "near misses" are on record in the U.S., including one "red alert" in which hundreds of Russian planes over Canada were finally determined to be a flock of geese on the radar screen. The commander of a single U.S. Trident II nuclear submarine will have at his command the capacity to destroy 408 different cities or other targets. Common sense, to say nothing of the Christian doctrine of man, argues against the folly of placing such destructive power in the hands of one fallible human being.

There is, nevertheless, an astounding degree of public apathy toward this unprecedented threat to life posed by the nuclear arms race. Whether from suppressed fear or ignorance, the common attitude seems to be one of avoidance: "A nuclear war will never happen." The unthinkable, however, is by no means impossible. Knowledgeable scientists at Harvard and MIT, as well as the highly respected Stockholm Institute for Peace Research, now predict that the proliferation of nuclear arms makes a nuclear war "inevitable" by 1999. Despite public apathy, there is good cause to wonder which will come first, the end of this century or the end of the world!

The extent of devastation in a nuclear war is difficult to estimate. Variables include the size of nuclear devices employed, altitude of detonation, force and direction of fallout-bearing winds, and the choice of military or civilian targets.[8] The following description of the aftermath of a nuclear war between the United States and the Soviet Union is based on studies published by the Congressional Budget Office and the U.S. Arms Control and Disarmament Agency:

> In the United States, around 120 million people are dead or dying. Seventy-five percent or more of U.S. industrial capacity is destroyed. Hundreds of cities are demolished. No significant military bases remain. In the Soviet Union, virtually all of 1300 military targets have been destroyed. About seventy per cent of Soviet industry is eliminated. From 60 million to 94 million people are dead or dying. In both countries, tens of millions more are injured. Medical care is almost non-existent and many more will die. Food and water are hard to find and the redistribution of supplies is impossible because of the destruction of all major transportation centers. Lingering radiation and damaging ultraviolet radiation from the sun (no longer screened out by an ozone layer in the atmosphere) make life for the survivors increasingly difficult and hazardous.[9]

The word "war" has become obsolete in the age of nuclear weapons. Today the accurate terms are holocaust, doomsday, apocalypse. Armageddon is no longer a figure of speech, nor the Book of Revelation a tract for other times. The biblical words of the Preacher are hauntingly relevant to the radioactive hell that follows in the wake of a nuclear configuration:

> "And I thought the dead who are already dead more fortunate than the living who are still alive; but better than both is he who has not yet been, and has not seen the evil deeds that are done under the sun" (Eccl. 4:2-3).

There can be no winners in a nuclear war. The fearsome quantities and qualities of weapons on both sides guarantee the suicidal result of such a conflict. Indeed, "Mutual assured destruction" is the stated Pentagon strategy and "MAD" its singularly appropriate acronym. "Mankind must put an end to the arms race, or the arms race will put an end to man." Every U.S. president since the beginning of the nuclear age has echoed this warning of John F. Kennedy. In defiance of both faith and reason, however, the race continues and escalates with ever increasing costs and risks. We believe the exigencies of geopolitics, economics, and technology are not sufficient in themselves to explain this malevolent compulsion toward a war in which everyone will lose.

A False Religion

This theological study is written with the firm conviction that the nuclear arms race is first and foremost a false religion. It is, to be sure, also bad politics, bad economics, bad science, and bad war. It can and should be opposed on all these fronts. To confront the motivating power of the arms race, however, to cut its vital nerve, the church must come to understand it theologically. Only with a biblical discernment can we unmask this threat to life, expose its evil nature, and name its many names.

A False Security

The fundamentally religious character of the nuclear arms race is seen first in its appeal to the human longing for security or, more precisely, its manipulation of that longing. As Abraham Maslow has shown, the human need to feel safe is a powerful motivator, second only to basic physical drives. The nuclear arms race and the wide-spread support or acquiescence it enjoys are founded on the illusion that security can be guaranteed by "strategic superiority," i.e., that salvation belongs to the strong. The certain sign of a false security, a false god, is the greater insecurity which inevitably results from its religious pretensions.

While the cry "national security" is raised to justify each escalation of the arms race, our nation and our world become progressively less secure. Each advance carries us not nearer the gates of heaven, but closer to the abyss. The very concept of defense has become outmoded in a nuclear-armed world. We have, in fact, no security against a nuclear attack. The U.S. National Security Council admits that if a button is pushed in the Kremlin, the Department of Defense will be powerless to save tens of millions of Americans from death in 20 to 30 minutes. We can only be assured that comparable numbers of Russian civilians will share our fate when retaliatory strikes are launched. The demonic nature of this false security is seen further in the global insecurity which it foments. Millions of Europeans know they will be caught in the nuclear crossfire, while the rest of the world awaits the inevitable, deadly fallout. Isaiah's word of judgment against a misplaced national security merits a careful hearing today:

> Woe to those who go down to Egypt for help
> and rely on horses,
> who trust in chariots because they are many

and in horsemen because they are very strong,
but do not look to the Holy One of Israel
    or consult the Lord! (Isa. 31:1)

A true measure of a nation's security is the quality of life within its borders rather than its power to wage wars beyond them. While a measure of defense is necessary in a fallen world, that nation is most secure whose citizens are adequately fed, housed, educated, employed, and cared for. In the United States, at present, approximately one-half of each tax dollar is spent to pay the debt on past wars or the cost of preparing for future war. It is ironic however, that the ire of the taxpayer is seldom directed toward the Pentagon. Military spending, expected to increase from 130 to 200 billion dollars annually during the 1980s, is itself the cause of growing insecurity in our society. Many economists warn that the procurement of military goods will continue to fuel inflation and exacerbate unemployment by creating far fewer jobs than similar expenditures in most areas of the civilian economy. Military research and development preempts one-third to one-half of the scientists and engineers in the U.S., thus inhibiting innovation in the civilian sector and giving the edge to Japan, West Germany, and other industrialized nations in the development and production of consumer goods. As the U.S. forges ahead in creating more effective instruments of death, it is falling behind in the capacity to produce the goods and services that offer a better life. "A country which, year after year, spends more then $100 billion annually to support a bureaucracy of four million people who produce nothing, and which buys hundreds of thousands of machines that make nothing is not on the road to prosperity."[10]

In a fundamental sense, security is a psychological and, even more, a spiritual quest. The Scripture warns repeatedly against the temptation to seek ultimate security in any proximate power, be it wealth, weapons, ideology, or the state. Ultimate security is not to be found in this world but in God who transcends the world while making himself known to his people in it. Security, then, is not the absence of threat. It is the presence of One who is "our only comfort in life and death," whose love casts out fear, whose power has overcome the powers of this world. "If God be for us, who is against us?" (Rom. 8:31). Paul's confident words were not penned in a fortress after a full meal, but in the midst of his life and death struggle with the opponents of the gospel he proclaimed.

In the biblical view, furthermore, security is never an end in itself or a prerequisite to the good life. It is always the result of life lived in right relationship to God and neighbor. The heart of the prophetic message of the Old Testament is that justice and righteousness, faith and obedience are the prior conditions for security in the land (Isa. 32; cf. Ezek. 34:27; Jer. 23:6; 33:16; also Lev. 25:18; Ps. 37:3). A nation's true security is to be found in the spiritual and ethical qualities of life, not in its many arms.

A False Morality

War has been a subject of the church's critical moral reflection in every age. The divine command against killing (Exod. 20:13) and Jesus' commands to love one's neighbor and not to resist one who is evil (Matt. 5:39-45) are a perennial challenge to Christian conscience in the midst of a fallen world. The early church espoused a pacifist position prior to the age of Constantine. While there is evidence that some Christians served in the Roman army, the ancient church fathers and other writers were unanimous in condemning Christian participation in war. Tertullian's comment, for example, is explicit: "Christ in disarming Peter ungirt every soldier."[11]

The Reformers feared anarchy more than tyranny. They upheld the right of the state to bear arms in order to deal with criminals and defend against enemy attack. Human depravity must be restrained, said Calvin, even by force if necessary. Righteous kings and princes are God's ordained minister of justice. Their use of weapons to defend the law and the people of their realm must not be abrogated by naive notions of human perfectibility which threaten the social order.[12] The Reformers, nevertheless, always cautioned restraint and considered war to be an act of last resort. Calvin wrote, "If they [the magistrates] must arm themselves against the enemy. . . . let them not lightly seek occasion to do so; indeed, let them not accept the occasion when offered, unless they are driven to it by extreme necessity. . . . Surely everything else ought to be tried before recourse is had to arms."[13] Luther's famous pamphlet, *Can Soldiers Be in a State of Grace?* is a witness to that Reformer's great reticence toward war and is, perhaps, a challenge to the modern church's easy conscience. One cannot appeal to human depravity or to the Reformation heritage as a sanction for indiscriminate or unrestrained warfare.

Calvin and Luther imposed careful restrictions on the conduct of war. They adhered to the "just war" theory formulated by Augustine and variously explicated during the medieval period. A just war must be a defensive response to unjustified aggression. Its goal is peace with the enemy. It must be conducted with restraint in a spirit of love rather than hate or vengeance. A just war requires careful discrimination between soldiers and non-combatants, protection of civilian populations, and humane treatment of prisoners. Wanton violence, massacre, atrocities, reprisals, or conflagration cannot be condoned. A hallmark of the just war theory is the principle of "proportionality," i.e., the good to be gained from a war must exceed the predictable evil which will result.[14] In short, war should be avoided. If unavoidable, it must be kept humane in order to preserve human society and conform to the will of God.

It is not the purpose of this paper to argue against every use of military force. One need not accept the pacifist position, however, in order to recognize the false morality inherent in any recourse to nuclear weapons. Ronald S. Wallace, a Calvin scholar, offers a noteworthy if understated speculation: "Judging by Calvin's language about war in his sermons it is possible that he might have been a pacifist in face of the possibility of modern nuclear war."[15] False religion leads to immorality as well as insecurity. Nuclear war and the preparations for it violate every code by which historic Christianity has determined a war to be just.

The simple weapons of the past could be adapted for the defense of a righteous cause, though their use was often horrible and seldom free from moral ambiguity. Nuclear arms, however, differ from those of the past not in degree but in kind. By their very nature, they make a just war impossible. The crucial moral distinction between combatants and non-combatants is obliterated. Nuclear warheads do not discriminate between soldiers and civilians, adults and children, guilty and innocent. Indeed, they exist to decimate an entire population. The possibility of defense which justified war in an earlier age no longer applies, while a retaliatory nuclear strike necessarily entails an act of wanton aggression against the innocent and the guilty in the homeland of the enemy. In the nuclear age, deterrence is nothing more than a massive hostage system with whole populations compelled to live under the constant threat of genocide. The word "restraint," so crucial to a Christian ethic of war, cannot apply when the act of war itself constitutes the ultimate lack of restraint. If massacre, atrocity, and conflagration are accepted as the very means of war, then moral choice and humane concern must surrender before the war is fought. There is no proportionality in the prospect of nuclear war. The incalculable evil which would result from such a conflict is immeasurably greater than any threat which these horrendous weapons are supposed to deter. No war can serve the interests of justice and peace if its methods in themselves are violations of God's law and crimes against humanity.

An eminent church historian has observed that "the more war has improved at the point of technology, the more it has deteriorated at the point of moral discrimination."[16] This deterioration approaches the point of moral disintegration when the citizens of a nation accept the premise that their sovereignty and security can justify the mass murder of innocents, the poisoning of the planet, the hideous mutation of the human species, and the possible destruction of all created life on earth. The church has never accepted the proposition that evil may be opposed by any possible means. Our fear of those who might kill the body must not drive us to accept the false security of weapons that jeopardize our souls.

Concerned people outside the chuch protest nuclear armaments because they are a threat to humanity. We concur. The chief reason for the church's opposition, however, is that such weapons are more than dangerous. They are idolatrous—an affront to God. Reformed theology emphasizes both the majesty of God and the ever present human propensity toward idolatry. Ultimate weapons, ultimate enemies, and ultimate ends that justify any means require a false god to sanction them. "If a man's moral values are the consequence of the God he worships, he will never change them without first changing gods. Until he does, all criticism of his standards will appear to him as treason."[17]

Idolatry is the investment of ultimate trust and value in any aspect of the created order. The biblical term "idol" is used in a literal sense to condemn the Baals and other "gods made with hands." Equally significant and more relevant to our time is the figurative extension of the meaning to include inordinate valuation of any proximate power, e.g., nature, wealth, weapons, or the state. God's sovereignty has never been universally acknowledged in a fallen world. Indeed, the essence of human sin is rebellion against divine authority and the desire to set up idols in God's place. Scripture teaches, furthermore, that the revolt against God's rule is so pervasive that it extends beyond the individual and human sphere of creation. This idolatrous rebellion has a corporate and cosmic as well as a personal dimension.

For we are not contending against flesh and blood, but against the principalities, against the powers, against the world rulers of this present darkness, against the spiritual hosts of wickedness in the heavenly places (Eph. 6:12).

The apostle Paul makes frequent reference in his letters to these "principalities and powers" which influence human life and are one important object of Christ's redemptive work (Rom. 8:38f.; 1 Cor. 2:8; 15:24f.; Eph. 1:20f.; 2:1f.; 6:12; Col. 1:16; 2:15). Although Paul's terminology is drawn from Jewish apocalyptic writings, modern scholarship has shown that his conception of the powers is quite different. Paul did not conceive these realities to be angels, spirits, or personal beings. He focused, rather, on the nature of the powers as superhuman, transpersonal realities that condition earthly life through the corporate order, structure, organization, and domination which they impose. Hendrikus Berkhof's seminal study, *Christ and the Powers,*[18] makes clear that Paul's thought can hardly be dismissed as mythology or superstition. It is the Word of God which sheds light on the complex social evils of our time!

Applying Paul's insight, Berkhof identifies several contemporary manifestations of the "principalities and powers": the state, politics, class, social struggle, national interest, public opinion, accepted morality, the ideas of decency, humanity, democracy, mammon, and military power.[19] A full treatment of Paul's concept of the powers is not possible here. The main lines of his thought should be noted, however, for they have direct bearing on our subject. First, it is clear that these powers are not inherently evil. The invisible structures of the universe, as well as all visible realities, were created "in, through, and for Christ" (Col. 1:15-17). The powers were created by God to give order and structure to human life, to divert chaos, and to bind humanity in fellowship with each other and with the Creator. Government, for example, is not evil in itself or a mere concession to human sin. Even in a perfect world, some political process would function by God's intent to make harmonious social life possible.

Paul notes, secondly, that the powers are fallen. Refusing to accept their proper role in the created order, the powers claim to be divine. They act as if they are the ultimate ground of being. They demand that ultimate loyalty be given to a party, a nation, a tradition, a race, or some other collective structure within the created order. Even in revolt, these powers fulfill a part of their original purpose. They do impose a kind of order that prevents chaos and makes corporate humanity possible. By claiming to fulfill that order in themselves, however, they lure humanity away from God rather than closer to him. "When Paul writes that nothing can separate us from the love of Christ, not even the powers, he presupposes that the nature of the powers would be to do just that, to separate us from love."[20] Finally, as we will consider below, the message of the gospel is that Jesus Christ, not the powers, rules the world! Through the crucifixion and resurrection, Christ not only acted to reconcile a lost humanity, he also "disarmed" the powers that oppress us (Col. 2:15).

Paul's discerning treatment of the powers sheds much light on the terrible reality of the nuclear arms race. Human fear or pride are not sufficient to account for this evil compulsion toward destruction, while mere goodwill and reason are clearly impotent to call a halt. We have no cause to doubt the sincerity of every U.S. president since Harry Truman. Each pledged to reduce this nation's nuclear arsenal. During the term of each, however, the stockpiles were inexorably increased. The nuclear arms race has taken on a life of its own, compelled by superhuman powers of evil that seem to defy the best human intentions. Indeed, we are not simply contending against flesh and blood. Any Christian attempt to disarm the nations must first expose these powers that dominate the so-called superpowers.

We must recognize, for example, the awesome power of technology. Our age embraces a technological determinism which assumes that because a new weapons system is possible, it is therefore desirable. The Poseidon must give way to the Trident, the ICBM to the MX—regardless of cost, actual need, or moral consequences. If we can build it, we must. The power of technology transcends the nations and holds each captive to fear. "If we do not create the next monster weapons, the enemy will. So we must do it first and on a grander scale." This same determinism explains why the persons who manage the technology of war need not consciously intend the mass slaughter of populations, the impoverishment of society, or the destruction of the planet. Technical language is carefully crafted to obscure and avoid the human consequences. Under this god, the truth is exchanged for a seductive lie (Rom. 1:25). Advances in death-dealing weaponry are not greeted with well-deserved horror. They are hailed as "progress," while a captive human ingenuity is blind to the distinction between technologically superior and morally worse.

The power of the profit motive also must be exposed. Mammon

has never lacked its legions of worshipers. The modern arms race serves its interests well. It is naive to assume that external threats alone can account for the unyielding momentum of the arms race. A continuing build-up of weapons, both conventional and nuclear, is immensely profitable for powerful vested-interest groups within the United States. Some economists refer to our "permanent war economy," in which millions of jobs and billions of dollars in profits are directly attributable to a growing weapons industry. The stock market has good reason to rebound when there is talk of war. In 1961 President Eisenhower warned against the growing power of the "military-industrial complex." Though largely unheeded, his words were prophetic. Today the Pentagon owns more land than the combined area of the six smallest states in this nation. It controls more wealth than the 15 largest corporations and utilities. Among American corporations, there are 22,000 prime defense contractors and 100,000 subcontractors,[21] each vying for a share in more than 50 billion dollars worth of military contracts awarded on a "cost plus" basis to private industry each year. The labor movement covets higher paying jobs generated by the weapons industry, while millions of individuals earn their living from the manufacture of war material. These corporate constituencies exert immense power in the political arena, investing large sums in campaign contributions and massive lobbying efforts to promote their interests in Congress. The logic of disarmament and peace is readily condemned as treason when so much profit accrues to so many through an economy of war. The military-industrial complex and its managers impel the arms race for profit. But they do not stand alone. The salaries of many Christians are paid, and many churches supported, by these same corporate revenues. Our American standard of living has come to depend on them. Thus we are all involved, however unwillingly, as the power of the bottom line edges humanity ever closer to the nuclear abyss.

Finally, we must recognize the demonic power of nationalism. "The pride of nations consists in the tendency to make unconditional claims for their conditioned values."[22] The truth of this assertion can be seen in the history of ancient Rome or Nazi Germany. It may be more difficult to recognize in the tide of current events. "National security" has become the watchword for the modern state's unconditioned claims. To justify any means including nuclear war the state must contend that its existence is to be equated with "freedom," "the future of the free world," or "western-Christian civilization." Among all the idolatrous powers, the state is particularly dangerous. Its unique power to inspire false worship is vividly portrayed in the description of the beast in Revelation 13 (especially v. 4; cf. Exod. 15:11). Individuals will not often lay down their lives for a technological improvement. Only rarely will they do so for a corporation. By millions, however, they will follow a flag into battle, especially when that flag is construed to represent not only a nation but the hope of the world. In making such idolatrous claims the state invariably oversteps the boundaries provided for it in God's order. It pretends to be God. Oscar Cullmann pronounces the biblical verdict on this national pride: "It is just this religious claim of the state that constitutes the satanic."[23]

Technology, mammon, and nationalism dominate modern life, offering false truth and a fraudulent security. Clearly, the fallen powers are beyond human control. We wrestle not with the flesh and blood but with the evil powers of security through might. Where mind and will must fall, faith may still overcome.

Disarming the Powers

"When Jesus was crucified and rose from the dead, and since then wherever this saving event is proclaimed, the domination of the world powers is at an end."[24] Christ has already accomplished what humanity in general and the church in particular are powerless to do. This good news is expressed most forcefully in Paul's letter to the Colossians:

> And you, who were dead in trespasses and the uncircumcision of your flesh, God made alive together with him, having forgiven us all our trespasses, having canceled the bond which stood against us with its legal demands; this he set aside, nailing it to the cross. He disarmed the principalities and powers and made a public example of them, triumphing over them in him (Col. 2:13-15).

The two effects of Christ's redemptive work stand side by side. First, the sinner is redeemed from personal sin and guilt. Secondly, the sinner is freed from bondage to the corporate powers of this age. Three different verbs are used to describe the fate of these powers in the face of the cross. Christ "disarmed" the principalities and powers by striking down their chief weapon, the illusion of ultimacy and righteousness. The cross reveals the awful truth about the powers. There Christ "made a public example" of them, for in the crucifixion their true nature was exposed. No longer can the powers claim to be god-like. When the true

Lord of the universe appeared, they did not serve him; they put him to death. Religion, morality, piety, law, the state, justice, and military power all conspired against the Son of God! Now the fallen nature of the powers is visible. Far from being god-like, they share none of God's wisdom, "for if they had, they would not have crucified the Lord of glory" (1 Cor. 2:8). Finally, writes Paul, Christ has "triumphed over" the powers by his cross and resurrection. This Greek verb refers to a Roman general's victory parade leading conquered rulers in triumphal procession through the streets of Rome. In the crucifixion, the powers did their worst, but it was not enough. The resurrection of Jesus Christ is the sign for all time that powers of this world are no match for the power of God.

This is not to say that if the gospel is preached, the powers will lay down their arms and submit. "In principle the victory is certain; yet the battle continues until the triumph will have become effective on all fronts and visible to all."[25] In the end Christ shall deliver the kingdom to God the Father "after dethroning every rule and every authority and power" (1 Cor. 15:24). Then the powers will be reconciled to their proper function as structures which serve God's intent for humanity. For the present they continue to seek headship for themselves. In the end they will be subjected to their true Head Jesus Christ (Eph. 1:10).

Thus, we live in that eschatological tension between the "already" and the "not yet," between "promise" and "fulfillment." Paul announces to the Colossians that Christ has disarmed the powers. He also asks them to remember his chains (Col. 4:8). The victory and the chains pose no contradiction. Those who share in Christ's triumph over the powers must also share in his struggle of suffering love against their domination. The powers have not surrendered. Indeed, their resistance intensifies now that their true nature is exposed. But for those who confess that "Jesus Christ is Lord," the power of the powers is already broken. That confession sets the limit to the powers. It de-deifies the cosmos. It declares the claims of the powers to be "un-self-evident." Free from bondage to the powers, the Christian is now able to see them in proper perspective. Berkhof writes: "We do not belong to the nation, the state, the technique, the future, the money, but all this is ours, given us by God as a means of living a worthy life before God and in fellowship with our neighbor."[26]

Paul's treatment of the powers culminates in a challenge to the church. The victory of God in Christ obligates the church to a special mission: "to make known the manifold wisdom of God to the princi-palities and powers in the heavenly places" (Eph. 3:10). Against the diverse machinations of the powers, the church bears witness to God's plan to unite all things in Christ (Eph. 1:10). Far from withdrawing from social life or politics, the church must "put on the whole armor of God" and stand against the wily, wicked rulers of this age. To be sure, all the weapons in this Christian panoply are defensive. Paul does not mention lance, spear, or bow and arrow (Eph. 6:10-18). The battle is Christ's not ours, and the victory is assured. This does not mean, however, that the church can give only a passive witness in the face of the evil powers. The earliest Christian confession, "Jesus is Lord," constitutes both a confession of faith and a political statement. It is an offense to the powers, and it inspires the church's peaceful offensive against them.

Christ's defeat of the powers is the source of the church's confi-dence in the face of social evils. It is decisive for Christian opposition to the most bizarre and threatening idolatry of our age.

> Only a Church which is alert and active in the struggle against the mor-tal enemy of mankind, who pretends to be a protector god, i.e., against armaments, only a Church which sincerely refuses to accept life from this mortal enemy, only such a Church is a Church of the untrimmed Gospel today![27]

A church that believes in the ultimate victory of Christ will incarnate the justice, mercy, and peace which that victory portends. Her life in community will transcend barriers of class, race, and nationalism. In the name of her Lord the church will foreswear allegiance to every ide-ology that divides and seeks to conquer through mistrust and fear. The church will stand against both an exploitative capitalism and an aggres-sive communism wherever these systems oppress humanity. The church will address the human need for security with care and compas-sion, exposing the danger of every false security, while proclaiming the good news that no powers can separate us from God's love in Christ.

The faithful church today will stand in the power of love against the false gods of this world. She will condemn any preparation or use of nuclear force and the godless morality of security through might. In-spired by a unit already manifested in Christ, she will call the nations to forge new, non-violent security systems based not on narrow nation-alisms but on the vision of global community and world order. A faithful church will resist runaway technology, rapacious profit motives, and the mad presumptions of the nations that compel the arms race.

Beyond preachments, platitudes, and position papers, the people of the churches must join in concrete acts of commitment to God's will for shalom. Rejecting the new war-winning technologies, we can encourage the contributions of science toward the new creation, such as the eradication of diseases, the alleviation of world hunger, and the harnessing of solar energy. Believing that a peaceful economy will prosper, we can work toward the conversion of the economy of war and seek ways to translate our faith into public policy. The people of God will be constant in prayer for a world in peril, interceding on behalf of the political and military leaders of powerful governments who must make the complex decisions which can lead to peace or war. Finally, the Christian will submit to the state and gratefully uphold its legitimate authority under God (Rom. 13:1). When the state oversteps its limits, however, advancing or defending idolatrous claims with ultimate weapons, the Christian must bow to the will of a higher Lord and "obey God rather than men" (Acts 5:29).

Christ has disarmed the powers. There is no doubt that they will be tamed. The question is no longer *if*, but *when:* before or after a nuclear holocaust. In this apocalyptic age the church must not succumb to apocalypticism. We live in hope. "We have tasted the goodness of the word of God and the power of the age to come" (Heb. 6:5). Empowered by this future hope, the faithful church will not shrink from its present witness. A clear "No!" to the nuclear arms race must be spoken. To disarm the nations we must wrestle with the powers that enslave them. To stand against these powers we must put on the whole armor of God.

Notes

1. Karl Barth, "Statement to the European Congress for Outlawing Nuclear Weapons," in *The Nuclear Challenge to Christian Conscience,* vol. 2: *The Response of Faith* (Washington, D.C.: *Sojourners Magazine*), p. 4.

2. Helmut Gollwitzer, "The Christian in the Search for World Order and Peace," in *Responsible Government in a Revolutionary Age,* ed. Z. K. Matthews (New York: Associated Press, 1966), p. 51.

3. Frank Barnaby, "The Mounting Prospects of Nuclear War: A Report of the Stockholm International Peace Research Institute," *Bulletin of the Atomic Scientists* (June 1977): 11.

4. Jim Wallis, "Nuclear War by 1999?" *Sojourners* (February 1977): 3.

5. Richard J. Barnet, "Challenging the Myths of National Security," *New York Times Magazine,* April 1, 1979, p. 58.

6. "The New Nuclear Strategy," *The Defense Monitor* (Washington, D.C.: Center for Defense Information), July 1976, p. 1.

7. Reported by NBC News, December 27, 1979.

8. Bernard T. Field, "The Consequences of Nuclear War," *Bulletin of the Atomic Scientists* (June 1976): 10-13.

9. "Two Scenarios for a Nuclear War," *The Defense Monitor* (Washington, D.C.: Center for Defense Information), March 1979, p. 4.

10. Barnet, op. cit., p. 60.

11. Roland H. Bainton, *Christian Attitudes Toward War and Peace* (New York and Nashville: Abingdon Press, 1960), p. 73.

12. John Calvin, *Institutes of the Christian Religion,* trans. Ford Lewis Battles, Library of Christian Classics, vols. 20-21 (Philadelphia: Westminster Press, 1960), IV.xx.10-11, pp. 1497-1500.

13. Ibid., pp. 1500f.

14. Bainton, op cit., pp. 96-97, 234.

15. Ronald S. Wallace, *Calvin's Doctrine of the Christian Life* (Grand Rapids: Wm. B. Eerdmans Publishing Co., 1959), p. 174.

16. Bainton, op. cit., pp. 245f.

17. E. LaB. Cherbonnier, "Idolatry," in *A Handbook of Christian Theology,* ed. Marvin Halverson, Arthur A. Cohan (Cleveland: World Publishing Co., 1958), p. 179.

18. Hendrikus Berkhof, *Christ and the Powers,* trans. John H. Yoder (Scottdale, Pa.: Herald Press, 1962, 1977).

19. Ibid., pp. 32, 49.

20. Ibid., p. 30.

21. Sidney Lens, "Mobilizing for Survival," *Washington Watch,* vol. 5, no. 47 (December 2, 1977).

22. Reinhold Niebuhr, *The Nature and Destiny of Man,* vol. 1: *Human Nature* (New York: Charles Scribner's Sons, 1964), p. 213.

23. Oscar Cullmann, *The State in the New Testament* (New York: Charles Scribner's Sons, 1956), p. 75.

24. Berkhof, op. cit., p. 36.

25. Ibid., pp. 39-40.

26. Ibid., pp. 40, 50.

27. Helmut Gollwitzer, "Our Struggle for Peace and Disarmament," unpublished paper read in West Berlin, September 20, 1977.

Affirming the United Church of Christ as a Just Peace Church

The United Church Of Christ

I. Summary

Affirms the UCC to be a Just Peace Church and defines Just Peace as the interrelation of friendship, justice and common security from violence. Places the UCC General Synod in opposition to the institution of war.

II. Background

The Thirteenth General Synod called upon the UCC to become a Peace Church and the Fourteenth General Synod asked a Peace Theology Development Team to recommend to the Fifteenth General Synod theology, policy and structure for enabling the UCC to be a peacemaking church. This pronouncement is based on insights from all three of the historic approaches of Christians to issues of war and peace—pacifism, just war, and crusade—but attempts to move beyond these traditions to an understanding rooted in the vision of shalom, linking peace and justice. Since Just War criteria itself now rules out war under modern conditions, it is imperative to move beyond Just War thinking to the theology of a Just Peace.

III. Biblical and Theological Foundations

A Just Peace is grounded in God's activity in *creation*. Creation shows the desire of God to sustain the world and not destroy. The creation anticipates what is to come: the history-long relationship between God and humanity and the coming vision of shalom.

A Pronouncement from General Synod 15

Just Peace is grounded in *covenant* relationship. God creates and calls us into covenant, God's gift of friendship. "I will make a covenant of peace with them; it shall be an everlasting covenant with them; and I will bless them and multiply them, and will set my sanctuary in the midst of them for evermore" (Ezek. 37:26). When God's abiding presence is embraced, human well-being results, or *shalom,* which can be translated *Just Peace.* A Just Peace is grounded in the reconciling activity of *Jesus Christ.* Human sin is the rejection of the covenant of friendship with God and one another and the creation and perpetuation of structures of evil. Through God's own suffering love in the cross the power of these structures has been broken and the possibility for relationship restored.

A Just Peace is grounded in the presence of the *Holy Spirit.* God sends the Holy Spirit to continue the struggle to overcome the powers ranged against human bonding. Thus our hope for a Just Peace does not rest on human efforts alone, but on God's promise that we will "have life and have it abundantly" (John 10:10).

A Just Peace is grounded in the community of reconciliation: the Just Peace *Church.* Jesus, who is our peace (Eph. 2:14), performed signs of forgiveness and healing and made manifest that God's reign is for those who are in need. The Church is a continuation of that servant manifestation. As a Just Peace Church, we embody a Christ fully engaged in human events. The church is thus a real countervailing power to those forces which divide, which perpetuate human enmity and injustice, which destroy.

Just Peace is grounded in *hope.* Shalom is the vision which pulls all creation toward a time when weapons are swept off the earth and all creatures lie down together without fear, where all have their own fig tree and dwell secure from want. As Christians, we offer this conviction to the world: peace is possible.

IV. Statement of Christian Conviction

A. The Fifteenth General Synod affirms a Just Peace as the presence and interrelation of friendship, justice, and common security from violence. The General Synod affirms the following as marks of a Just Peace theology:
  • Peace is *possible.* A Just Peace is a basic gift of God and is the force and vision moving human history.

- The *meaning* of a Just Peace and God's activity in human history is understood through the Bible, Church history, and the voices of the oppressed and those in the struggle for justice and peace.
- Non-violent *conflict* is a normal and healthy reflection of diversity; working through conflict constructively should lead to growth of both individuals and nations.
- *Nonviolence* is a Christian response to conflict shown to us by Jesus. We have barely begun to explore this little-known process of reconciliation.
- *Violence* can and must be minimized, even eliminated, in most situations. However, because evil and violence are embedded in human nature and institutions, they will remain present in some form.
- *War* can and must be eliminated.
- The *State* should be based upon participatory consent and should be primarily responsible for developing justice and well-being, enforcing law and minimizing violence in the process.
- *International structures* of friendship, justice and common security from violence are necessary and possible at this point in history in order to eliminate the institution of war and move toward a Just Peace.
- *Unexpected initiatives* of friendship and reconciliation can transform interpersonal and international relationships, and are essential to restoring community.

B. The Fifteenth General Synod affirms the UCC as a Just Peace Church. The General Synod affirms the following marks of a Just Peace Church, calling upon each local church to become:
  - A community of hope, believing a Just Peace is possible, working toward this end, and communicating to the larger world the excitement and possibility of a Just Peace.
  - A community of worship and celebration, centering its identity in justice and peacemaking and the Good News of peace which is Jesus Christ.
  - A community of biblical and theological reflection, studying the Scriptures, the Christian story, and the working of the Spirit in the struggle against injustice and oppression.
  - A community of spiritual nurture and support, loving one another and giving one another strength in the struggle for a Just Peace.

- A community of honest and open conflict, a zone of freedom where differences may be expressed, explored, and worked through in mutual understanding and growth.
- A community of empowerment, renewing and training people for making peace/doing justice.
- A community of financial support, developing programs and institutions for a Just Peace.
- A community of solidarity with the poor, seeking to be present in places of oppression, poverty, and violence, and standing with the oppressed in the struggle to resist and change this evil.
- A community of loyalty to God and to the whole human community over any nation or rival idolatry.
- A community without enemies, willing to risk and be vulnerable, willing to take surprising initiatives to transform situations of enmity.
- A community of repentance, confessing its own guilt and involvement in structural injustice and violence, ready to acknowledge its entanglement in evil, seeking to turn toward new life.
- A community of resistance, standing against social structures comfortable with violence and injustice.
- A community of sacrifice and commitment, ready to go the extra mile, and then another mile, in the search for justice and peace.
- A community of political and social engagement, in regular dialogue with the political order, participating in peace and justice advocacy networks, witnessing to a Just Peace in the community and in the nation, joining the social and political struggle to implement a Just Peace.

C. The Fifteenth General Synod affirms friendship as essential to a Just Peace.
   1. We affirm the unity of the whole human community and oppose any use of nationalism to divide this covenant of friendship.
   2. We reject all labeling of others as enemies and the creation of institutions which perpetuate enemy relations.
   3. We affirm diversity among peoples and nations and the growth and change that can emerge from the interchange of differing value systems, ideologies, religions and political and economic systems.
   4. We affirm non-violent conflict as inevitable and valuable, an

expression of diversity and essential to healthy relationships among people and nations.

5. We affirm all nations developing global community and interchange, including:
   a. freedom of travel;
   b. free exchange of ideas and open dialogue;
   c. scientific, cultural, and religious exchanges;
   d. public education which portrays the other nations fairly, breaking down enemy stereotypes and images;
   e. knowledge of foreign languages.

D. The Fifteenth General Synod affirms justice as essential to a Just Peace.

1. We affirm all nations working together to insure that people everywhere will be able to meet their basic needs, including the right of every person to:
   a. food and clean water;
   b. adequate health care;
   c. decent housing;
   d. meaningful employment;
   e. basic education;
   f. participate in community decision-making and the political process;
   g. freedom of worship and religious expression;
   h. protection from torture;
   i. protection of rights without regard to race, sex, sexual orientation, religion, national or social origin.

2. We affirm the establishment of a more just international order in which:
   a. trade barriers, tariffs and debt burdens do not work against the interests of the poor and developing nations;
   b. poor nations have a greater share in the policies and management of global economic institutions.

3. We affirm economic policies which target aid to the most needy: the rural poor, women, nations with poor natural resources or structural problems, and the poor within each nation.

4. We affirm economic policies which will further the interests of the poor within each nation:
   a. promoting popular participation;

     b. empowering the poor to make effective demands on social systems;

     c. encouraging decentralization and greater community control;

     d. providing for the participation of women in development;

     e. redistributing existing assets, including land, and distributing more equitably future benefits of growth;

     f. reducing current concentrations of economic and political power;

     g. providing for self-reliant development, particularly in food production.

5. We affirm nations transferring funds from military expenditures into programs which will aid the poor, and developing strategies of converting military industries to Just Peace industries.

6. We oppose the injustices resulting from the development of national security states that currently repress the poor in organizing society against an external enemy.

7. We affirm a free and open press within each nation, without hindrance from government.

E. The Fifteenth General Synod affirms common security from violence as essential to a Just Peace.

1. We affirm that national security includes four interrelated components:

     a. provision for general well-being;

     b. cultivation of justice;

     c. provision for defense of a nation;

     d. creation of political atmosphere and structure in which a Just Peace can flourish and the risk of war is diminished or eliminated.

2. We affirm the right and obligations of governments to use civil authority to prevent lawlessness and protect human rights. Such force must not be excessive and must always be in the context of the primary responsibility of the state in creating social justice and promoting human welfare. Any use of force or coercion must be based in the participatory consent of the people.

3. We affirm that war must be eliminated as an instrument of

national policy and the global economy must be more just. To meet these goals, international institutions must be strengthened.

4. We affirm our support for the United Nations, which should be strengthened developing the following:
   a. more authority in disputes among countries;
   b. peacekeeping forces, including a permanent force of at least 5,000, able to police border disputes and intervene when called to do so by the U.N.;
   c. peacemaking teams, trained in mediation, conflict intervention, and conflict resolution;
   d. support for international peace academies;
   e. a global satellite surveillance system to provide military intelligence to the common community;
   f. international agreements to limit military establishment and the international arms trade;
   g. an international ban on the development, testing, use, and possession of nuclear and biochemical weapons of mass destruction;
   h. an international ban on all weapons in space and all national development of space-based defense systems and Strategic Defense Initiatives.

5. We affirm our support for the International Court of Justice and for the strengthening of international law, including:
   a. the Law of the Sea Treaty;
   b. universal ratification of the International Covenants and Conventions which seek to implement the Universal Declaration of Human Rights;
   c. recognition of the jurisdiction of the International Court of Justice and removal of restrictions, such as the Connally Amendment, which impair the Court's effective functioning.

6. We reject any use or threat to use weapons and forces of mass destruction and any doctrine of deterrence based primarily on using such weapons. We also reject unilateral full-scale disarmament as a currently acceptable path out of the present international dilemma. We affirm the development of new policies of common security, using a combination of negotiated agreements, new international institutions and institutional power,

non-violent strategies, unilateral initiatives to lessen tensions, and new policies which will make the global economy more just.

7. We affirm the mutual and verifiable freeze on the testing, production, and deployment of nuclear weapons as the most important step in breaking the escalating dynamics of the arms race, and call upon the U.S. and the U.S.S.R., and other nations to take unilateral initiatives toward implementing such a freeze, contingent upon the other side responding, until such time as a comprehensive freeze can be negotiated.

8. We declare our opposition to all weapons of mass destruction. All nations should:
   a. declare that they will never use such weapons;
   b. cease immediately the testing, production and deployment of nuclear weapons;
   c. begin dismantling these arsenals;
   d. while the process of dismantling is going on, negotiate comprehensive treaties banning all such future weapons by any nation.

9. We declare our opposition to war, violence, and terrorism. All nations should:
   a. declare that they will never attack another nation;
   b. make unilateral initiatives toward dismantling their military arsenals, calling upon other nations to reciprocate;
   c. develop mechanisms for international law, international peacekeeping, and international conflict resolution.

General Synod 15 Proposal for Action: Organizing the United Church of Christ as a Just Peace Church

I. Summary

Affirms the UCC to be a Just Peace Church and defines Just Peace as the interrelation of friendship, justice and common security from violence. Places the UCC General Synod in opposition to the institution of war.

II. Background

This Proposal for Action builds on the proposed Pronouncement, also submitted to the Fifteenth General Synod, "Affirming the United Church of Christ as a Just Peace Church." Like the Pronouncement, the Proposal for Action has been developed in response to the request of the Fourteenth General Synod to recommend theology, policy, and structure for enabling the UCC to be a peacemaking church.

III. Directional Statement

The Fifteenth General Synod calls upon all in the United Church of Christ to recognize that the creating of a Just Peace is central to their identity as Christians and to their Baptism into the Christian community.

IV. Call to Local Churches

The Fifteenth General Synod calls on local churches to organize their common life so as to make a difference in the achieving of a Just Peace and the ending of the institution of war.

The Fifteenth General Synod calls for the development of four key components within local churches: spiritual development, Just Peace education, political advocacy and community witness:

1. We call all local churches to the inward journey of spiritual nurture: prayer for a Just Peace, study of the Scriptures, theological reflection upon the work of the Holy Spirit, celebration and worship which center the life of the community in the power and reality of the God who creates a Just Peace. We call for the development of Christian community which nurtures and supports members in the search for a Just Peace. We commend to all local churches the use of the World Peace Prayer, using the example of the Benedictine Sisters who pray this specific prayer each day at 12 noon:

    Lead me/us from death to life, from falsehood to truth.
    Lead me/us from despair to hope, from fear to trust,
    Lead me/us from hate to love, from war to peace.
    Let peace fill our hearts, our world, our universe.

2. We call all local churches to the inward journey of education. Knowing that there are no easy answers to the creating of a Just Peace, we call for churches to establish the climate where all points of view can be respected, all honest feelings and opinions shared in the search for new answers and directions. We call for a steady program of Just Peace education, a steady flow of information on Just Peace issues into the life of the congregation.

3. We call all local churches to the outward journey of political witness, enabling all members to join the search for the politics of a Just Peace. Just Peace is both a religious concept and a political concept, and participation in the political arena is essential. We call for each church to appoint a contact person for the UCC Peace Advocacy and Hunger/Economic Justice Networks to follow closely those political issues most critical to the development of a Just Peace and to alert members of the local church when it is most appropriate to write or contact their Senators and Representatives.

4. We call all local churches to the outward journey of community witness. We call for local churches to make their convictions known in their communities through public forums, media, and presence in the public arena. We call for local churches to help shape public opinion and the climate in which the issues of a Just Peace are shaped. We call for churches to explore with military industries the opportunities for conversion into Just Peace industries. We call for evangelistic outreach, inviting others to join in the search for a Just Peace.

Because the times are so critical, we call for extraordinary witness as well as ordinary political involvement to break the power of the structural evils which prevent a Just Peace. We call upon local churches to be understanding and even supportive of persons who out of individual conscience take the responsibility for such non-violent extraordinary witness. Examples of such witness might include: becoming a conscientious objector to war; refusing acceptance of employment with any project related to nuclear and biochemical weapons and warfare; refusing any and all assignments to use weapons of mass destruction as a member of the military; withholding tax money in protest of the excessively militaristic policies of our government; and engaging in acts of non-violent civil disobedience, willingly going to jail to call attention to specific outrages.

V. Call to Conferences and National Bodies

The Fifteenth General Synod calls upon Conferences and national bodies of the UCC to organize their common life so as to make a difference in the achieving of a Just Peace and the ending of the institution of war.

The Fifteenth General Synod calls for the development of four key components in developing the United Church of Christ so that it can make a real difference over the next years: regional centers, Washington advocacy, international presence, and national programs.

1. We call upon Conferences to develop regional centers able to link local churches into effective regional and national strategies. A variety of options are possible at the Association and Conference levels:

    • The development of regional UCC peace centers that resource local groups through educational, organizational, advocacy, and funding efforts;

    • The development of ecumenical regional Just Peace centers, in partnership with other denominations;

    • The funding of part-time contract, or full-time Just Peace staff at the Association or Conference;

    • The funding of ecumenical peace staff in states or metropolitan areas.

2. We call for the strengthening of our advocacy work in Washington, D.C., with more funding to develop the capacity of the UCC to make its witness known in the national political arena, to expand its capacity for policy analysis, to increase its presence on Capitol Hill in shaping legislation, to develop stronger communication links with churches around the country to share political developments and urge action, and to build coalitions.

3. We call upon the United Church of Christ Board for World Ministries to explore and develop new models of peace and justice ministries globally to address particular situations of injustice, oppression and real or potential violence, and to develop communication links between Christians in these critical situations and Christians in the U.S., developing global partnership and global awareness in the search for a Just Peace.

4. We call upon all national bodies to continue to develop effective programs of advocacy, empowerment, and education. We call for more resources to develop national strategies of advocacy and ac-

tion to increase the witness of the UCC for a Just Peace. We call for the Office for Church in Society to facilitate the coordination of this work.

VI. Implementation

Churches, Conferences, and national bodies, including the Office for Church in Society, the Executive Council, the United Church Board for World Ministries, and the Stewardship Council, have been requested in this Call to Action to respond to various directions. These bodies are responsible for developing the strategies and programs to fulfill the goals outlined here.

Perspectives on Education, the State, and Religion

The State as an Established Religion

James Tunstead Burtchaell

Congress shall make no law respecting an establishment of religion, or prohibiting the free exercise thereof.

There have been few altercations between church and state in America which did not somehow bring into play this portion of the First Amendment to the Constitution. That is not to say that the relations of the civil government to religion have consistently followed the convictions and purposes of the framers of the Bill of Rights, murky and elusive though those purposes are to our later view. Quite the contrary, it would appear that those purposes have often enough been unravelled by later judicial interpretation.

Parliamentary history in Great Britain had long been antagonized by religious disputes over tithes for the clergy of the Established Church, revisions in the Prayer Book, the orthodoxy of the Articles of Faith, the outlawing and then the toleration of some forms of religious dissent, struggles between the Lords Spiritual and the Lords Temporal, and between the Convocations of Canterbury and York and the Parliament, and such like. The American statesmen wanted free of all that. Article VI of their Constitution had forbidden religious tests for civil office, and the amendment was to go further still.

The Establishment Clause restrained the general government from establishing a single national church or from interfering in other ways with the provisions that the various states had made for religion. It also provided that any subsidies which the Congress might give to religious institutions must be given without favoritism between the churches. The U.S. Supreme Court overturned these original purposes in *Everson v. Board of Education* (1947) when it held for the first time that religion could not be favored over irreligion, and that the Fourteenth Amend-

89

ment had extinguished the original provision of the First Amendment to leave the states free to make their own decisions about the treatment of religion. The court relied on the writings of James Madison to reconstruct the intention of the First Congress which had framed the amendment, but as Michael Malbin has shown, it overlooked the evidence of the congressional debates which record the final text as having emerged from a compromise in which Madison had had to yield considerable ground to his colleagues.

The Free Exercise Clause seems to have been intended to protect religious opinion and belief, and perhaps worship, but not to draw a cloak of privilege over all religious speech or activity. In a series of cases, however (*Braunfield v. Brown* [1961], *Sherbert v. Verner* [1963], and *Wisconsin v. Yoder* [1972]), the clause lately has been construed to make religious tenets a constitutional ground for exemption from the observance of civil and criminal law.

Thus the Establishment Clause has been narrowed: it is no longer read to allow governmental subsidies to church institutions. At the same time the Free Exercise Clause has been broadened: it now immunizes religious action as well as religious thought from the obligations of civil law.

There have been other mutations, equally curious. The two clauses originally had been issued as parallel and complementary. In effect, the one protected the people from a national tithe and the other from a national dogma. But modern jurists have put them into tension against one another. The one is thought to make the state aloof from the churches and the other to make the state deferential to them. Further, the authors originally had intended an even-handed but firmly secular amiability. All citizens, whatever their faith, must conform to the laws; all churches, whatever their citizen support, might be beneficiaries of the state. More recently an animus against all religious faith has reversed the sense of the amendment by alienating the state from the aspirations of the churches and by estranging believers from the authority-claims of the state.

It would be incomplete and uninteresting to study the relations of church and state in America merely by following the fate of the First Amendment at the hands of its interpreters. For these jurists themselves, like the framers before them, have been caught up in a larger contention, and they partake of broader beliefs, convictions, and debates to which even the First Law of the land is eventually subject. It is to that larger theater of thought that we should turn. In our own time one can discern a growing momentum of opinion on this issue of church and state that may bear heavily on both our minds and our laws, and may be nudging both lives and laws onto a course quite other than the bearings given us in the First Amendment.

The Public Good

It has become conventional for us to describe as "public" only those activities which are managed by the state. Detroit Street and Railways is thus called public, because it is run by the city government. And American Airlines is called private, even though it carries people on their travels and transports their mail for the U.S. Postal Service. Cook County Hospital is public, and Presbyterian–St. Luke's is private; yet each of them serves the same health needs of the people. The Smithsonian Institution is public and the Metropolitan Museum of Arts is private. Brandeis and Saint Olaf and Southern Methodist are private, while Wayne State and CUNY and Annapolis are public.

But on the contrary it should be clear that, whether they be for profit or not-for-profit, whatever their funding, whatever their governance, all these institutons serve the people's welfare. All of them are truly public in that most basic sense. The governments direct some of them, while others are governed by trustees who represent either the stockholders or the public. All are for the people. Our reluctance to call them "public" derives from a totalitarian assumpton that only the civil government can be politically responsive to the people, and therefore only the state can be trusted to provide for the people's general needs.

By this same wisdom which sees the state as the only fit patron of public institutions, the First Amendment's provision for religion is seen to be perfectly reasonable because religion is viewed as a most private enterprise. Faith is taken to be an individual conviction grounded on no premises that are discussable in open society, and hence need be no concern of the public welfare.

But this is to misunderstand. The Constitution exempts religion from state governance not because it is private but because there are some public enterprises quite essential to the commonweal that should on no account lie under the command of the government. The press and public speech and religion are all given similar freedoms from restriction, not because thay are private goods but because they are public goods that cannot survive state control.

Speech, publication, and religion have this in common: they all deal in ideas. It is the state's business to wield coercive power to assure the observance of the law and the fostering of the common welfare. That one area of the common welfare where the politically applied power of coercion does little good and much harm is the area that withers unless allowed its freedom: the area of the intellect, of research, of judgment, of the mind's adventure. Thus, while the state may be the public's good servant in supervising justice, it is a poor protector of the truth.

The very people who gave us the First Amendment had a clear idea that is was appropriate for the state to collaborate with other institutions for the public welfare . . . including the churches. During the same year that the First Amendment was drafted, debated, and enacted by the Congress (1789), the Northwest Ordinance was reenacted. It provided that schools were to be built with federal assistance on federal lands, schools that were virtually all run by churches: "Religion, morality, and knowledge being necessary to good government and the happiness of mankind, schools and the means of learning shall be forever encouraged." Years before the states of the Union undertook to found schools, and centuries before the federal government involved itself in funding education nationwide, the opportunity to learn was provided to the territorial public by schools that were, for the most part, religious. Does the appearance of state schools later then deprive those older foundations of their public character, and rob them of their original relationship to the people? Here, in the very drafting room of the First Amendment, the authors of the great clauses were lending financial subsidy and recognition of public character to religious institutions they were unwilling to govern but which they saw as appropriate co-agents for the common good.

That precedent raises a question for whoever is disposed today to claim for the state a monopoly on providing for the public welfare.

Tax Relief: A Gift or an Acknowledgment by the State?

When the government allows for tax relief in favor of other public enterprises, is this an allotment by the state from its wealth, or is it a deferential allowance for the need for other public institutions? This is a test, in the practical order, of whether or not the state must be the master of any enterprise for it to be truly public.

Several years ago the Congress was debating a bill to offer a modest federal tax credit for expenses incurred in the education of children at independent schools. Legislators were eventually persuaded not to support the proposal because it would be supportive of religious schools and therefore constitutionally assailable. The same session, however, enacted a tax credit for expenses incurred in the installation of insulation in family homes, because such measures would redound to the public welfare by reducing fuel consumption. Rockwool was for the public good, but religiously affiliated education was not.

More recently, the U.S. Supreme Court upheld a Minnesota law which made some educational expenses deductible from taxable income. The decision was much criticized because the pupils destined to benefit most were enrolled in religious schools, which the *New York Times* called "privileged, private enclaves." Meanwhile day-care and baby-sitting expenses were deductible, and no complaints were heard. All Saints School is for private benefit; Donald Duck Daycare is for public benefit.

What principle lies behind this criticism? It is difficult to assign it to anything but consistent antireligious bias. Church schools have always operated at a lower per-pupil cost (usually between one-third and one-half the costs of state schools). They presently function well in disintegrating inner-city neighborhoods where state schools have collapsed.

Parents who prefer religiously sponsored schooling are obliged to accept severe financial penalties. First, they pay their school taxes like other citizens. Second, they receive no educational benefits from those taxes. Third, because they are paying but not benefiting, the school taxes of the other citizens are thereby lowered. Fourth, they then pay the fees to have their own children educated. Fifth, they pay further taxes on the money used to pay those fees. Sixth, because of all those disparities they cannot afford to pay those who teach their children in religious schools nearly what the state school teachers earn. When these parents who bear such an accumulation of costs simply because they want their children to have what they regard and what the First Congress regarded as a comprehensive education—when these parents occasionally request an arrangement that is less unfair, they are told that it is only right for them to be penalized because it is deviant and un-American to draw their children out of the only schools that serve the truly public good.

This is a matter toward which Catholics are particularly sensitive, for most of that bias with respect to schools has been directed specifically at us, who have the heaviest investment of any religious community in education. But beneath that hostility is another viewpoint that merits our attention.

The legitimacy of any tax exemption, deduction, or credit is grounded on that American belief that the common good is best secured by a mixture of institutions, ventures, and investments, not all of which ought to be controlled by the state. Because parental responsibility for education is seen to take precedence over that of the government, and because education is a matter of the mind (which we as a free people have always been reluctant to put too tightly into the grasp of rulers), it is one of those areas wherein a state monopoly may not be desirable. And if this is so, then tax arrangements should incorporate that belief.

The classical theory of taxation has held that individual citizens and groups of citizens should be encouraged to give their money to support beneficial works, and that the taxing arm of the government ought to respect these eleemosynary gestures as possessing a dignity and a discretion that is prior both in right and in history. Thus, when the government accedes to these individual gestures toward the common good, it is not simply handing *its* money over to the citizens for their private preferences. It is acknowledging that the citizens reserve to themselves some allotments to the public welfare prior to the claims of the government. The money is first of all the property of the citizens.

That theory is being challenged by a newer belief: that all money of all citizens is rightly available to the state; that the government may in the past have failed to exercise its right to tax some monies being devoted to "charitable purposes"; but that, because the government has a much wiser view of what the nation's social needs really are (since our rulers stand upon the peaks, and citizens scan things only from the lowlands), it is now time to call in those previously privileged dollars and put them to better public use.

The tax-break controversy brings to light in a slightly different way a fundamental question. Do the people have—by right—the option of supporting other institutions which to their mind render important services to the common good, and which can do so precisely because they are not of the state? And if this be so, is the government to acquiesce in it as a gesture of indulgence, or is this a popular right that claims priority over the government?

Is the State the Source or the Acknowledger of Family and Church Prerogatives?

One of the classical defenses by the Christian church against civil totalitarianism has been the claim that the church has a warrant of authority that need not yield to the commands of the state, for the church does not derive from the state nor should it be subject to it. The church claims to be another public institution. Those who are not disposed to acknowledge that claim might nevertheless be sympathetic to a similar claim made on behalf of the family. And for some time under our republic the family was respected as having an authority the state did not confer but could only acknowledge.

This issue was raised directly in *Pierce v. Society of Sisters* (1925), in which the respondents were the order of nuns for whose elementary school education I remain grateful today. In defense of its challenged law that required all children to attend state schools, Oregon had argued:

> If the governments of the several states have no power to provide for the education of the children within its limits, and if the character of the education of such children is to be entirely dictated by the parents of such children, or by those persons by whose influence the parents are controlled, it is hard to assign any limits to the injurious effect, from the standpoint of American patriotism, which may result. . . .
>
> Our children must not under any pretext, be it based upon money, creed or social status, be divided into antagonistic groups, cliques, or cults there to absorb the narrow views of life as they are taught.

The Supreme Court struck down that law because it abridged "the liberty of parents and guardians to direct the upbringing and education of children under their control."

> The fundamental theory of liberty upon which all governments in this Union repose excludes any general power of the state to standardize its children by forcing them to accept instruction from public teachers only. The child is not the mere creature of the state; those who nurture him and direct his destiny have the right, coupled with the high duty, to recognize and prepare him for additional obligation.

Forty years later the court pursued the same line of thought when it struck down a state law forbidding the use of contraceptives. It held, in *Griswold v. Connecticut* (1965): "We deal with a right of privacy older than the Bill of Rights—older than our political parties, older than our school system."

Here was acknowledgment that the ancient bonds between parent and child, husband and wife, had a certain priority over the civil law itself. The state was not the creator of the family, and the state held itself bound to sustain familial bonds insofar as the people wished it so. And for their wisdom on this matter it was understood that the people might turn to other institutions than the state.

But this was not a view that would continue into our own times. In 1972, in *Eisenstadt v. Baird,* the Supreme Court held that unmarried people had as much right to obtain and use contraceptives as did the married: "If a right of privacy means anything, it is the right of the individual, married or single, to be free from unwarranted governmental intrusion into a matter so fundamentally affecting a person as the decision whether to bear or beget a child." The privilege of privacy was now transmuted from a right of the family to a right of the individual apart from family.

Soon the court went further and asserted that the right of privacy the state was obliged to protect was the privacy of an individual *against* the family. In a series of cases (*Bellotti v. Baird* [1979], *H. L. v. Matheson* [1981], *City of Akron v. Akron Center for Reproductive Health* [1983]) the court decided that a physician was henceforth free to abort a minor without the consent or even the knowledge of her parents, if she were mature before the law; if legally immature, she might ask an agent of the state to act instead of her parents. Parental interests therefore must give way to what the government sees as the minor child's interests. And in *Planned Parenthood of Central Missouri v. Danforth* (1976) the court went far in another direction. It struck down a law that supported the right of a husband to participate in any abortion decision made by his wife: "The State cannot delegate authority to any particular person, even the spouse, to prevent abortion."

With *Danforth* the tradition had come all the way around. Any rights and claims between family members must now depend upon delegation by the state. Instead of the state acknowledging primeval status and rights within the family, the family must now look to the state as the source and arbiter of its rights. This mutation was not dissimilar to what had befallen the interpretation of the First Amendment. Originally both church and family had been acknowledged as institutions with which the state must reckon, with a dignity that deserved respect and support from the civil law, and with relations to their members that enjoyed a privacy and some immunity from state regulation. As things later stood, both church and family lost the power to establish relationships the state ought to honor or support. Thus, the privacy enjoyed among these societies was suppressed in favor of a new privacy—individual instead of corporate—which citizens were to enjoy and for which they would receive state protection: a privacy *from* the church and *from* the family, rather than a privacy *within* them.

Here, it seemed, the state had been transformed from an ally of church and family into a jealous rival.

State and Church as Rivals in Social Service

Yet another way the state has recently come to impinge upon the exercise of religion is in the area of social services. When the Constitution was written, government—particularly the federal government—was not expected to address itself to the economic, educational, domestic, corporal, or cultural needs of the people. Other agencies and organizations ministered to these: mostly under religious motivation and sponsorship. Quite recently it has become accepted practice for the government to supply most of the systemic support for social welfare. As a previous secretary of HEW said over a decade ago, this immense political change has transformed "the task of aiding life's victims from a private concern into a public obligation."

His description of the change illustrates again the pervasive conviction that only government sponsorship can render an operation truly public. The statement would be accurate if one identified the churches, the Red Cross, the Sierra Club, the American Cancer Society, and tens of thousands of hospitals, juvenile homes, mental health centers, colleges, asylums, hospices, child care facilities, retirement homes, and other enterprises which the people have founded for their human needs as "private" simply because they are not managed by the government.

When the government does enter a field of social services as an entrepreneur, several scenarios become possible. In the first, the government becomes a competitor. Its taxing power renders it a doubly formidable one. A government agency can and usually does have access to more lavish funding than the previously existing religious or independent agencies. Also, the fact that their constituencies have already been taxed to pay for these governmental facilities now makes it especially difficult for the other institutions to appeal to them for support to keep their own operations going. Yet it is perhaps this very disparity of affluence that has allowed many religiously sponsored services to continue more effectively, because their personnel operate with a different motivation. The risk, however, is that governmental competition will crowd most other social agencies out of existence.

In the second scenario, the state may subsidize other agencies to allow them to function alongside its own. But then, on the supposition that "neutrality" must attend the expenditure of any tax dollar, and that neutrality is a charism possessed by itself but not by any church, the government begins to pressure the subsidized agencies to discontinue anything that smacks too much of religious faith and dedication. Or it attaches conditions to its subsidy that have the same effect: they bleach out of the service operation the character and personal commitment that no government can command, and that preserve the credibility and compassion that make the operation more humane.

The churches are thus held in a terrible dilemma. If the government decides to enter a field of service where they have been actively ministering, they will either be forced to vacate a field because they can no longer afford to operate there, or be forced to forfeit their autonomy and motivation and operate as government subsidiaries. It sometimes seems that they must be either bankrupted or secularized.

When the government wishes, it is quite capable of moving into a sector of social service leaving the existing operations autonomous and supported. This has been the case, for instance, in foster care of children, distribution of foodstuffs in impoverished countries, and health care. That it has been obviously not the case in the entire field of education raises the thought that the formation of minds is an enterprise in which the state is particularly sensitive about religiously sponsored competition.

Political Effects of Religious Teaching

There is a further rub between church and state that may have begun to chafe more in recent times, though it is a very ancient irritation. Religious leaders have always been ready to teach their followers what their duties were in matters regulated by the state. Parliamentarians have been no less nervous than princes at the prospect of facing a constituency that has been effectively coached by religious teachers.

This matter has not yet come to crisis before our judiciary. The Supreme Court has repeatedly held—recently in *McGowan v. Maryland* (1961) and *Harris v. McRae* (1980)—that no law violates the Establishment Clause merely because it coincides with the tenets of a particular religion. But the court has yet to face the sharper question of whether a law that was provably enacted because religious leaders called for it is unconstitutional.

The modern resentment of religious teaching that impinges on the political process does not derive from the jurists. Some of it is simply displaced political resentment. The electoral clout of certain fundamentalist television preachers is disdained by those who find fault with their Christian theology, by those who find their political applications too conservative, and by those whose churches do not have a comparably resonant teaching (either because they have a decentralized polity or because they lack effective media presence). Instead of criticizing the preachers on those grounds, the critics tend merely to say that the opinions of religious officers have no place in politics.

Some activists in the political order have used the accusation as a debating point. The National Abortion Rights Action League, for example, decided at the outset that they must identify a villainous force as their opponents, because the policy the league wanted to sponsor was repugnant to a majority of the population. They settled on the Catholic bishops, not because the bishops had been outspoken on the subject of abortion but because they were a group most easy to discredit. That these organizers have achieved so much success is evidence of the American public's distrust of religious teachings that lead to any particular moral and political choice.

Sometimes the accusation against preachers meddling in politics is motivated by a disagreement over the issue. The point of procedure is raised only when partisans believe they have been unsuccessful in convincing the public of the merits of their own position. Thus doctrinaire liberals who worked closely with Catholic leaders on legislation for conscientious objection, immigration policy, farm labor rights, racial integration, and welfare reform became uncharacteristically indig-

nant when these same Catholic leaders disagreed with them over abortion. Now all prolife political activism is denounced as priestcraft and
dogma.

In the face of this public uneasiness religious leaders have tended
to step gingerly. But they may be ignoring a very important issue. What
kind of preaching would they be offering if their congregations did not
form from it some very solid convictions about the common good and
about how to provide for it politically? The very ability of religious
leaders to convey such convictions reminds us that insofar as the laws
and policies of the state are free to reflect the convictions of the people,
they must lie open to the influence of those whose judgment and teaching is effective with that people. This is perhaps the point of sharpest
jealousy and vulnerability for partisan political leaders. It is surely the
reason why the church is either coerced or co-opted or opposed in totalitarian regimes, for rulers there cannot abide leaving the political
process open to anyone's preaching but their own.

The State as an Established Religion

The First Amendment was enacted by men who believed the state
would be better off untrammeled by the responsibility to govern a
church. It is just possible that events have brought those two great societies into a new and stressful situation. It is possible that in our time the
state is in danger of being established as a national religion.

There is a tendency in the minds of our fellow Americans to look
to the state for the plenitude of their needs. All rights flow from the state,
all other societies look there for their legitimacy, all public concerns are
addressed through it, all resources lie under its claim, all social under-
takings can be confiscated by it as under eminent domain, all wisdom
about the people's welfare must come there for adjudication.

As for the church, its leaders are mesmerized by the state. Poverty,
injustice, greed, enmity, gluttony, dishonesty—all the ancient nemeses:
the church at times appears to have no further strategy of defiance in
the face of them than to get a better appropriation passed or to lobby
for a better law. Clergy by the thousands have departed the pastoral ministry and been ordained by HHS or HUD.

It is wearying but expectable to see the churches hectoring the
government because they are unsatisfied with its record of service. But
it is positively alarming to suspect that with a little bit of improvement

here or there, and some programmatic adaptations to suit their national policy committees, the churches might actually reach the point of satisfaction, for want of any agenda beyond what the government might incorporate into its platform.

Perhaps it is timely now for the church once again to enact a few of its basic beliefs. This time it might be well to provide that the church shall not reduce its gospel to such dimensions as could be established by the state, nor ever expect that the free exercise of faith could truly be realized, let alone stifled, by any state.

What, Then, of Religious Schools in a Democratic and Pluralistic State?

From a Christian perspective, we can view the school issue simply as one instance of church-state relations. Christians' obedience to the rule of God in their lives sometimes collides with the claims of their civil rulers, and the prerogative to educate has naturally been a jealous interest of both state and church.

For most controversialists, the very way in which they choose to describe their conflict may be a prime way of asserting their position. One account may call this a contest between church and state. Each society is sovereign over its own concerns, and jurisdictional disputes are resolved by deciding whether a given matter is in the sacred or the secular sphere. Another explanation, radically different, may see the limited authority of civil rulers in contest with the unlimited lordship of God. The sacred and the secular overlap—indeed, they co-penetrate—since our service to our fellow humans is secular in its activities yet sacred in motivation and eternal significance.

This same stress is well exhibited in the long debate in America about the schooling of youth. State education, like many other eleemosynary institutions (hospitals, orphanages, hospices, homes for the elderly), was originally founded under church auspices. And, like most of these public services, most schools have since been transferred to state management and governance. Some believe, however, that there is still good reason for schooling to continue also under publicly Christian auspices. Hospitals existed not simply because there were afflicted persons needing medical treatment and care but because it behooved Christians to embody their faith in the ministry of healing. Likewise for the schools: some believe that beyond scholarly inquiry and teaching there is a passing-on of wisdom and perspective that Christians owe one another, integrated with all else that they are learning.

This is one church-state issue, however, on which American Christian bodies have not been of one mind. In our national past the lines have not been drawn simply between active Christians and their critics. Christians have been divided among themselves. Protestants have typically regarded church schools as divisive, and have favored the state system as democratic, pluralist, and free. Catholics have typically found the state schools to be, in fact, Protestant, and have sought their freedom in schools of their own. Protestant documents, including some from Presbyterian authorities, have both attacked Catholic schools as subversive of national unity and called for the disentanglement of state schools from all religious doctrines or observances, lest the growing population of Catholics enable them to take over the schools and impose their own dogmatic regimen. Catholics replied, in some heat, that a Protestant majority so dominant as to be unconscious of itself had already made the state schools effectively and offensively sectarian, and that in any case the American solidarity was not truly threatened by the internal loyalties and doctrines of the several churches.

That much is history. It would be a misleading guide to the situation today. There are more than three million students in Catholic schools today. But much more significant may be the fact that an estimated 85 percent of Catholic students are enrolled in state and other independent schools. In 1983 more freshmen in college identified themselves as Catholics (39 percent) than all Protestants combined (32 percent). Catholics clearly have a massive stake in the soundness of the state educational effort.

On the other hand, lest anyone imagine that the churches of the Reformed and Presbyterian tradition are uniformly negative toward church schools, we must note that they have 106 affiliated colleges and universities of their own. Some of these churches have long maintained hundreds of primary and secondary schools; and local congregations are now beginning to found such schools in some denominations where it has not hitherto been the tradition.

It is simply not the case, then, that Catholics have a vested interest only in church schools and Protestants have an interest only in the state schools. The debate, if debate it continues to be, does not follow denominational lines as once it might have.

Among Presbyterians and Reformed and Catholics alike, it is acknowledged today that educational choices are primarily entrusted to parents, not to officials of either church or state. What the churches can do is agree that the state ought to ensure those choices are truly accessible: not only legally, but practically.

Another view common today is that American society is and will continue to be religiously pluralist. We are all beneficiaries of the civil freedoms our communities enjoy here under law. And we know that pluralist societies must be provided by their governments with pluralist institutions. Thus a vigorous network of state-provided schools where no American or guest need feel estranged or alien is a national need that we are together in acknowledging.

If we ought to join in any concern about state schools, it is not that they lack religious neutrality. It is that the only practical strategy of neutrality has been to delete religious perspective and consideration altogether.

Some see this embargo on religious tradition and wisdom as an aggressive and purposeful establishment of secularism, whose dogma that religious faith is irrational and counterscientific is simply a new form of sectarianism, no less authoritarian for its want of a sponsoring church. On this view, the state schools have come under an ideological orthodoxy that is hostile to all religious commitment or perspective. Faith is not simply absent: it is banished and disdained. It is not mentioned, it may not be mentioned, and the implication is that it is not worth mentioning.

Another estimate of contemporary state schools says that they offer no ideology at all. That must be a deficiency for Christians who regard as incomplete and deceptive any account of truth that does not raise the questions or integrate the perspectives and wisdom of the faith community.

Thus, the previous concerns about real or possible capture of the state schools by one or another religious regimen have been replaced by a new set of concerns: the schools either offer no interpretive viewpoint at all, or offer one which purposely embargoes all references to faith. Be these schools non-sectarian or sectarian (for secularism too can be a sectarian dogma), many Christian parents are unsatisfied with them as an only alternative. A true pluralism, they claim, must offer a plurality of choices, at least as regards a service for which they have already paid so heavy a tax.

The state might better be charged to promote education than to be only a provider. One would hope that there be no true constitutional impediment to prevent the state from subsidizing more even-handedly the education of the nation's young in schools of their parents' choice. These schools should offer a quality of instruction that satisfies the kind of norms that are appropriate to civil purview. If Presbyterian institutions can withhold social security payments from their employees' income and transmit them to the state; if Catholic patients can be admitted to Jewish hospitals for treatment subsidized by Medicaid—then the children of all should be able to find an educational alternative that is integrated with their religious quest and commitments and sustained by their educational taxes.

Education is of concern to both the civil society and the believing communities. One policy has insisted that when church and state have coincident interests one must either control or exclude the other. More authentic would be a relationship less combative, though still wary. Pluralism has been protected by a single strategy: neutrality. Surely impartiality could be a supplementary strategy.

Christians should be committed to a national polity that honors people of every faith as full compatriots. And we should be persuaded that a love of God which is prior to love of neighbor, but is verified and embodied in love of neighbor, is a higher loyalty the state must accommodate.

Recent Opinion on the Religion Clauses of the First Amendment: A Background Study for Discussion of Government Impingement of Religious Liberty

Anne Ewing Hickey

In reflecting on the thrust of our present dialogue—government impingement of religious liberty—I wondered on what basis this sentiment has gained currency as an expression of social reality. The evidence in the forefront for fundamentalists decrying the apparent godless secularism of American society as well as Christians worried about the eclipse of their traditions into a private, trivialized realm would likely be the now famous school prayer decisions of the Supreme Court in the 1960s. My general impression of the Supreme Court's action in these decisions was that it had moved rather thoughtlessly in the direction of the increasing secularization of American society. Aware that my thoughts were impressionistic rather than informed, I decided that a study of the religion clauses of the First Amendment to the Constitution was a basic prolegomenon to reflection on the presence or absence of religious liberty in American society in general and in the realm of education in particular. This study, therefore, is an attempt to highlight some of the constitutional parameters set on the role of religion in public life by reference to the theoretical justification for such limitations in the recent opinions of the Supreme Court of the United States on the religion clauses of the First Amendment. Needless to say, this is very much in the nature of an overview, offered as a guideline, and not as a comprehensive account. The inclusion of reflection on the constitutional parameters set on the role of religion presupposes a delicate relationship between political and religious liberty, the preservation of which cannot be taken for granted.

I. Introduction

*Congress shall make no law respecting an establishment of re-
ligion, or prohibiting the free exercise thereof.*

The genius and the dilemma of the constitutional provisions for the
place of religion in American public life is that there are two clauses
which can and often do conflict with one another. Ellis West, in his dissertation on the conflict between the two religion clauses of the First
Amendment, cited the comments of innumerable legal scholars on the
dilemma posed by the fact that each clause carried to a logical extreme
could in many instances impinge upon the other.[1] The competing values
of the right to freely exercise one's religion and the right to avoid being
subject to an establishment of religion have posed highly complex issues to the Supreme Court in recent years, resulting in decisions that
often appear to have no uniform theoretical framework. The complexity of the court's task in sorting through the competing issues of free
exercise and disestablishment in landmark cases such as *Everson v.
Board of Education* (1947), *Abington School Dist. v. Schempp* (the
school prayer case), and the very recent *Lynch v. Donnelly* (the munic-
ipal creche display case) should warn us against facile views of the
place of religion in society based exclusively on religious zeal or a
simplistic understanding of church/state separation.

The history of the formulation of the religion clauses of the First
Amendment figures prominently in the Supreme Court's development
of constitutional theory and resolution of particular cases and, according to some scholars, provides a key to much of the ambivalence about
the meaning of a prohibition against establishment of religion. During
the formation of our nation Patrick Henry and George Washington supported an effort to make all Christian churches the established church
of the State of Virginia on an equal basis; it was defeated by the separationist sentiment of Thomas Jefferson.[2] And it was Jefferson who
penned the phrase "a wall of separation between Church and State"
which was, beginning with *Reynolds v. United States* (1878), to gain
the ascendancy as an interpretive summary of the religion clauses of
the First Amendment.[3] However, the Jeffersonian theory that "a wall of
separation" should stand between the church and the state was not, according to Mark De Wolfe Howe, the only theoretical impetus to the
First Amendment in the eighteenth century.

Perhaps, very suggestively for our purposes as people whose identity is grounded in religious faith, there was, Howe argues, a theological principle of separation that was at least as formative of the First Amendment as was Jefferson's.[4] In *The Garden and the Wilderness,* Howe sets forth the thesis that the Supreme Court has misapprehended history in emphasizing the Jeffersonian theory of separation as the interpretive key to the religion clauses, when Roger Williams's more theological doctrine of separation had great currency in the eighteenth century.[5] According to Howe the Jeffersonian theory was rooted in an anticlerical bias and saw the "wall of separation" as functioning to prevent the state from becoming an instrument of ecclesiastical aims.[6] The more theological principle of separation, which Howe calls "the evangelical principle," was based on the believer's concern that government will intrude into the religious realm and thereby taint its freedom and authenticity.[7] Roger Williams used the Jeffersonian metaphor of "wall" to image the line between church and state but viewed it from the perspective of the spiritual concern for the privacy necessary to holiness rather than the political concern for the privacy necessary to freedom:

> When they have opened a gap in the hedge of wall of separation between the garden of the church and the wilderness of the world, God hath ever broke down the wall itself, . . . and made this garden a wilderness.[8]

Howe argues that "the evangelical principle" of separation, which had great currency at the time of the writing of the First Amendment, sought privileges for religion, viewing disability but not favor as violative of the principle of separation.[9]

While Howe, writing in 1965 shortly after the school prayer decisions, faulted the Supreme Court for neglecting this more religiously sympathetic view of separation, James Kirby, writing in 1976 in the *North Carolina Law Review,* faults Howe for overlooking another strand of constitutional history that finds a theoretical basis for separation apart from maintaining the privacy necessary for spiritual holiness and political freedom. Kirby adds to the Jeffersonian and Williams strands the justification for separation articulated by James Madison— the avoidance of religio-political strife.[10] According to this theory, government neutrality in the religious arena is essential to social harmony, for it precludes hostility between religious factions, who would compete for governmental favor. Kirby argues that neutrality, understood theoretically as essential for the avoidance of religious strife, became important for the Supreme Court's decisions on establishment issues in the 1970s.[11]

These three perspectives on the theoretical justification for and meaning of separation between church and state, all of which scholars claim have roots in constitutional history, have informed the Supreme Court's recent decisions on cases involving the religion clauses of the First Amendment and may account for recent decisions which appear to a layperson such as myself to lack consistency. Henry Abraham, writing in the *Journal of Church and State* in the spring of 1980, argued that the court has articulated three principles of separation of church and state that appear to me to be extensions of these three historically rooted strands: (1) strict separation, e.g., the logic but not the decision of *Everson v. Board of Education, McCollum v. Board of Education* (1948), and *Engel v. Vitale* (1962), the first school prayer case; (2) government accommodation, e.g., *Zorach v. Clauson;* and (3) government neutrality, e.g., *Abington School Dist. v. Schempp,* the second school prayer case.[12]

II. The Free Exercise Clause

Because the intent of the free exercise clause of the First Amendment appears to have posed a less complex interpretive problem to the Supreme Court than the establishment clause, I shall take it up for discussion first. Most of the case law on the religion clauses of the First Amendment is of quite recent origin. The first case before the Supreme Court on the question of religious liberty was in 1845,[13] but it wasn't until the 1940s when the protection of the First Amendment was found applicable to state law as well as federal that the court had enough cases to develop a legacy of church-state relations based on case law.[14] Beginning with the Jehovah's Witnesses cases (fifteen between 1938 and 1946),[15] case law on the meaning of the free exercise clause seemed to be moving in a consistent enough direction for Henry Abraham to write in 1980 that the last decade had seen a "commendably ascending commitment to a maximum regard for free exercise."[16]

The most dramatic recent evidence of the health and vitality of the constitutional commitment to the right to freely exercise one's religion in American society is the decision in the case known as *Wisconsin v. Yoder et al.* (1972). All of us who bemoan the court's seeming preference for secularism can take heart at the sensitivity to religious values expressed in this decision. The Supreme Court sustained the claim of the Old Order Amish that compliance with the compulsory school attendance law impinged on their right to free exercise of religion.

The importance of this decision warrants closer scrutiny of the written opinion. The Amish argued that sending their children to a public high school in accordance with the compulsory attendance law of Wisconsin was in conflict with their religious beliefs, which require careful community tutelage after the eighth grade.[17] The Amish brought in expert witnesses who testified that not only was this regulation an impingement of the Amish right to free exercise, it also threatened the survival of the religious sect.[18] Chief Justice Burger, writing for the majority, agreed with the Amish claim. In this case, he wrote, there was not "a state interest of sufficient magnitude to override the interest claiming protection under the Free Exercise Clause."[19]

Unfortunately for sectarian movements of recent origin, the decision seemed to hinge largely on the legitimacy and survivability of the Old Order Amish as demonstrated by their history.[20] Further, despite their seeming eccentricity, the Amish had proven themselves to be responsible citizens who had created a self-reliant community that posed no burden on society.[21] Perhaps an unspoken, or even unconscious, basis for the granting of this special privilege was that the loss to the state was minimal.

Whether the trend most dramatically demonstrated in *Wisconsin v. Yoder,* i.e., the exempting of groups from compliance with general legislation on free exercise grounds, will continue may be an open question. Jesse Choper (professor of law, Berkeley), writing in *The Supreme Court: Trends and Developments* (1981–82), noted that the current court when faced with a similar case drew the line on legislative exemptions with the tax question.[22] In 1982 an employer, who was Old Order Amish, refused to pay social security taxes on his employees' wages, citing free exercise claims.[23] The court found that in this case, unlike the *Yoder* case, the state had a compelling interest in compliance with the general legislation whether it conflicted with religious scruples or not.[24] Further evidence that religious liberty, when in conflict with general legislation, may not always enjoy the privileged position promised by the *Yoder* case is found in Justice Stevens's separate concurring opinion in the Amish's battle with social security. Stevens argued that special exemptions for religious reasons are not really required by the free exercise clause and may in fact be a tilt toward unlawful establishment.[25]

III. The Establishment Clause

Interpreting the establishment clause of the First Amendment has posed a highly complex problem to the arbiters of constitutionally acceptable policy and legislation, resulting in decisions that seemingly fit no consistent theoretical framework for understanding the meaning of establishment of religion. Legal scholar Henry Abraham thinks the complexity stems from the three distinct and competing views of separation of church and state (strict separation, neutrality, and accommodation)[26] that arguably have roots in constitutional history and gain ascendancy depending upon the composition of the court. Or perhaps it is the close interweaving of national ideology and Christianity in American history that disallows clear distinctions between secular and sectarian and, consequently, prompts the paradox of finding the following statement articulated by the paradigmatic liberal justice William O. Douglas, writing for the majority:

> We are a religious people whose institutions presuppose a Supreme Being. . . . When the state encourages religious instruction or cooperates with religious authorities by adjusting the schedule of public events to sectarian needs, it follows the best of our traditions.[27]

Whatever the source of the constitutional ambiguities about what role religion can play in public life without violating establishment principles may be, I will not attempt here to provide an analysis of the overarching theory or political development that might explain the jagged path taken by the Supreme Court in recent decisions on religion in public life. Rather, I will review some of the most significant decisions in order to uncover the competing values at work in American society and reasoning of the justices in giving precedence to a particular value in a particular fact situation.

Everson v. Board of Education, 330 U.S. 1 (1946), is the landmark case of recent history for interpreting the establishment clause and is, so to speak, the spring from which all other decisions flow. The paradox of the case that points toward future ambiguities with regard to governmental aid to religion is that aid to parochial schools is found constitutionally acceptable within the framework of a strictly separationist opinion.[28] The incompatibility of the theoretical reasoning with the consequent decision has resulted in the subsequent citing of the case by opposing sides of the question of state aid to religion.[29]

The fact situation of the case is as follows. A board of education in

New Jersey authorized reimbursement for school children riding public transportation to school, either public or non-profit private.[30] A taxpayer in the New Jersey district filed suit claiming that such an authorization of tax money to a church-related school violated the establishment clause of the First Amendment. In a split decision, the majority found that this type of indirect aid to religious education was constitutionally acceptable. Writing for the majority, Justice Black articulated an often-quoted definition of the meaning of the parameters set on religion by the establishment clause:

> The "establishment of religion clause" of the First Amendment means at least this: Neither a state nor the Federal Government can set up a church. Neither can pass laws which aid one religion, aid all religions, or prefer one religion over another. Neither can force nor influence a person to go to or to remain away from church against his will or force him to profess a belief or disbelief in any religion. No person can be punished for entertaining or professing religious beliefs or disbeliefs, for church attendance or non-attendance. No tax in any amount, large or small, can be levied to support any religious activities or institutions. . . . In the words of Jefferson, the clause against establishment of religion by law is intended to erect a "wall of separation" between Church and state.[31]

The opinion, in a moment of prescience, noted the potential clash between the establishment and free exercise clauses and implied that this consideration was significant for the decision.[32] Black argued that the First Amendment does not prohibit a general policy of aid which inadvertently benefits a religious group.[33] To do so would amount to discrimination against a religious group and potentially impinge upon their free exercise rights.[34] This is not to say that New Jersey could not set forth a policy benefiting public school children exclusively, but they are not required to do so by establishment prohibitions.

Justice Jackson, dissenting, noted the discord between the theory of separation of church and state articulated by the court and its decision and, unlike the majority, followed through the separationist logic in his dissenting conclusion that "Catholic education is the rock on which the whole structure rests, and to render tax aid to its Church School is undistinguishable to me from rendering the same aid to the Church itself."[35]

The internal discord in the *Everson* decision between separationist theory and accommodationist result may explain the contradictory results of the next two important Supreme Court decisions on the constitutionality of religious instruction (not liturgical activity) in the public schools. *McCollum v. Board of Education* and *Zorach v. Clauson* both involve what were called released time instructional programs of a religious nature. The specifics of the cases are so similar that it is difficult for the layperson to understand why the outcomes should be so different. In *McCollum*, religious instruction was offered on a voluntary basis to public school children and was held on public school grounds in a classroom. This was found to violate the establishment clause. The only distinction in the subsequent case, *Zorach*, was that the instructional program was not held on school property. Justice Douglas, writing for the majority, held that in view of the fact that the religious instruction in the *Zorach* case was held off school property, and cost the taxpayer nothing, it did not violate the establishment clause simply to adjust the public school schedule to the religious needs of the pupils.[36] In what would become the ground of the accommodationist view of the relation between church and state,[37] Douglas argued that there is no historical precedent requiring government to be hostile to religion. Rather, historical precedent allows for governmental accommodation to the religious needs of the people within establishment limits:

> But we find no constitutional requirement which makes it necessary for government to be hostile to religion and to throw its weight against efforts to widen the effective scope of religious influence. The government must be neutral when it comes to competition between sects. . . . But it can close its doors or suspend its operations as to those who want to repair to their religious sanctuary for worship or instruction.[38]

When the Supreme Court rendered its momentous decisions on prayer in the public schools in the early 1960s, the legacy of the *Everson, McCollum,* and *Zorach* cases on the question of constitutionally acceptable religious activity in public schools was one of confusion and ambiguities. Louis Pollak, writing in the *Harvard Law Review,* argued that the first of the two school prayer decisions did nothing to cut through the ambiguities to a clear guideline for distinguishing acceptable and unacceptable religious activity in the public arena.[39] However deficient in terms of predictive significance, the opinion in *Engel v. Vitale* is, nonetheless, clear in its opposition to the form of school prayer under consideration.

The New York State Board of Regents, the governmental agency charged with overseeing the state's public school system, recommended that the following prayer that they had composed be repeated each day by the school children in the presence of the teacher:

> Almighty God, we acknowledge our dependence upon Thee, and we beg Thy blessing upon us, our parents, our teachers and our Country.[40]

The prayer, as is apparent, was non-denominational, and the recitation was made voluntary.

Justice Black, writing for the majority, found that the policy of the New York Board of Regents violated the prohibition against establishment of religion:

> We think that the constitutional prohibitions against laws respecting an establishment of religion must at least mean that in this country it is no part of the business of government to compose official prayers for any group of the American people to recite as a part of a religious program carried on by government.[41]

Justice Black stated that it didn't matter that the prayer was non-denominational and voluntary. Free choice is illusory in this case, for the weight of governmental sanction brings to bear indirect, if not direct, coercion:

> When the power, prestige and financial support of government is placed behind a particular religious belief, the indirect coercive pressure upon religious minorities to conform to the prevailing officially approved religion is plain.[42]

Justice Black, in buttressing his opinion, pointed out that the trend toward establishing churches in the colonies (the Church of England was initially established in Maryland, Virginia, North Carolina, South Carolina, and Georgia)[43] was thwarted by the Founding Fathers, who valued religious liberty more dearly than a particular religiosity.

In summary, Justice Black's opinion on the unconstitutionality of the New York Regent's prayer focused on the fact that it was composed and implemented by governmental authorities and that, as such, it posed a threat to religious liberty as protected by the establishment clause.

Justice Stewart wrote the sole dissenting opinion in which he staked out the ground on establishment issues that would come to fruition in a lengthy dissent in the next school prayer case. Stewart saw re-

ligious traditions as inextricably linked with national heritage and the
severing of the two as a loss of national authenticity:

> I cannot see how an "official religion" is established by letting those
> who want to say a prayer say it. On the contrary, I think that to deny the
> wish of these school children to join in reciting this prayer is to deny
> them the opportunity of sharing in the spiritual heritage of our Nation.[44]

In the next major school prayer case, official propagation of religious beliefs is further limited and a theoretical framework for determining whether legislation or policy is constitutionally acceptable
within establishment limits began to evolve. In *Abington School Dist.
v. Schempp*, the landmark school prayer decision, the State of Pennsyl-
vania by law had required that the public schools begin their day with
the reading of ten Bible verses, but any child having a written request
from his/her parent could be excused.[45] The Schempp family, who were
Unitarians, filed suit to prevent the school district from requiring such,
claiming it was an establishment of religion. The program objected to
included the reading of ten Bible verses, if possible over the intercom
(if not by the teacher), without comment, followed by the recitation of
the Lord's Prayer in unison by the school children.[46]

Writing for the majority, Justice Clark held that the religious prac-
tices in question violated the establishment clause, and articulated the
concept of "wholesome neutrality" as the interpretive key to the meaning of the religion clauses of the First Amendment. Beginning with
Schempp, according to legal scholar Ellis West, the court began moving
away from the language of "separation of church and state," which, of
course, is nowhere in the Constitution, to the language of neutrality.[47]
Justice Clark argues that the neutrality required of the government in
matters religious does not allow it to let the majority use the machinery
of the state to advance its views.[48] This does not impinge on the majority's right to free exercise, for free exercise does not include the privilege of imposition.

Justice Brennan wrote a lengthy (eighty-page!) concurring opinion in the *Schempp* case, the heart of which, according to legal scholar
Louis Pollak, is the thesis that liberty guaranteed by the Constitution
allows the American parent a choice for his/her children between a
secular education imbued with democratic values or a sectarian education steeped in different values.[49] The inclusion of daily religious exercises by statute in the public schools is of recent origin (the statute in

the *Schempp* case dating to 1913) and is not a right provided to parents as part of their guaranteed liberties.[50]

Justice Stewart, once again the sole dissenter, wrote a dissenting opinion in which he argued that the parents who wished to have religious exercises for their children in public school had a strong free exercise claim. In a paragraph that bears attention despite its length, Stewart views the exclusion of religion from public life as a kind of discrediting and handicapping that hinders the free advancement of religion:

> It might be argued here that parents who wanted their children to be exposed to religious influences in school could, under Pierce [*Pierce v. Society of Sisters,* 268 U.S. 510], send their children to private or parochial schools. But the consideration on which renders this contention too facile to be determinative has already been recognized by the Court: "Freedom of speech, freedom of press, freedom of religion are available to all, not merely to those who can pay their own way." . . . A compulsory state educational system so structures a child's life that if religious exercises are held to be impermissible activity in schools, religion is placed at an artificial and state-created disadvantage.[51]

In *Schempp,* the desire of some to pay homage to a Supreme Being in the context of a public educational setting collided with the right of others not to have an official version of religion imposed upon them. However important the preservation of the religious dimension of our national heritage may be, according to *Schempp* it is not government's role to advance religious beliefs no matter how denominationally bland or allegedly volitional. While the court in *Wisconsin v. Yoder* allows for exemptions from legislation in order to allow for free exercise, it did not in *Schempp* provide for the converse, i.e., an exemption from legislation which a minority found to tend toward establishment. Interestingly, the collision of values in *Schempp* was not between secular and religious values, for the offended party was a Unitarian family.[52] Rather, the collision was between two versions of religion, only one of which had official sanction.

According to Ellis West, *Schempp* was the first step in a movement toward the articulation of a clear theoretical framework for interpreting what governmental activity violated the establishment clause. The language of "wholesome neutrality" used by Justice Clark would become the interpretive key to understanding the intent of the religion clauses.[53] The court, according to West, has not used the language of separation of church and state as determinative of the outcome of a case since 1976.[54] The "wholesome neutrality" of *Schempp* that required the government surrogate, the school system, to stay out of the business of propagating religious beliefs evolves into the "benevolent neutrality" of *Walz v. Tax Commission* (1970) that allows the government to exempt church property from taxation.[55] According to West, the "benevolent neutrality" concept of the meaning of church/state separation is based on the recognition that absolute neutrality is impossible in view of the pervasive character of modern governmental bureaucracy.

According to West, the direction of the Supreme Court in the 1970s was to carry the concept of neutrality in a more concessionary direction. However, there was a measure of discipline brought to the constitutionality of government accommodation to religion by means of a theoretical framework for guiding establishment decisions—the so-called primary purpose and effect test.[56] Justice Clark, in *Schempp,* articulated the first part of this three-pronged test. What is the primary purpose and primary effect of a piece of legislation? According to *Schempp,* in order to be compatible with First Amendment guarantees legislation and policy must have a secular purpose and a primary effect of neither aiding nor inhibiting religion.[57]

The "purpose and primary effect test" of *Schempp* was further refined by the plumbline of "excessive government entanglement" criterion of *Lemon v. Kurtzman.* The logic of what is called the Lemon test[58] is as follows: If a governmental policy has a secular purpose and a primary effect of neither aiding nor harming religion but secondarily does so, it still does not violate the First Amendment unless it involves the government in excessive entanglement with religion.[59]

Whatever order and stability had been brought to the determination of what government activity constitutes establishment by the so-called Lemon test has, according to some commentators, been shaken by the recent Pawtucket creche display case, *Lynch v. Donnelly.*[60] Not only does the court, according to Justice Brennan's scathing dissent,[61] apply the Lemon test in a very superficial fashion, Justice Burger, writing for the majority, boldly claims that the court is not limited to this test.[62]

The *Lynch v. Donnelly* case bears scrutiny because of its timeliness in reflecting the views of the recent court on the question of establishment and constitutionally permissible religious activity on the part of government. In a 5-4 decision, the Supreme Court on March 5, 1984, held that the city of Pawtucket, Rhode Island, had not violated the establishment clause of the First Amendment by including a nativity scene in their Christmas display in the center of the shopping district. The most significant aspects of the opinion seem to me to be the use of the word "accommodation" as a key phrase for describing the intent of separation between church and state and the provisional commitment to the Lemon test, which had evolved into a reasonably clear guideline for determining establishment.

Chief Justice Burger, writing for the majority, critiques a slavish devotion to the Jeffersonian metaphor "wall of separation."[63] While useful as a reminder that the establishment clause prohibits an established church, the metaphor does not reflect current social reality where no institution exists in a vacuum.[64] Burger invokes the language of "accommodation" as an alternative to "wall of separation" as the interpretive key to the religion clauses:

> Nor does the Constitution require complete separation of church and state; it affirmatively mandates *accommodation,* not merely tolerance, of all religions, and forbids hostility toward any. . . . Anything less would require the "callous indifference" we have said was never intended by the Establishment Clause. . . . Indeed, we have observed, such hostility would bring us into "war with our national tradition as embodied in the First Amendment's guaranty of the free exercise of religion."[65]

Burger justifies the accommodationist posture by reference to the fact that the same week that the establishment clause was approved Congress provided for a congressional chaplain.[66] He calls the tradition of congressional chaplains a "striking example of the *accommodation* of religious belief intended by the Framers [of the Constitution]."[67]

Burger uses the language of "accommodation" once more in the opinion in the context of a summary of numerous examples of governmental recognition of the religious dimension of our national heritage that have not been found to violate establishment principles: "evidence of accommodation of all faiths and all forms of religious expression, and hostility toward none" is the keynote of American history.[68]

The opinion of the majority seems to hinge on its view that the creche, despite the religious significance of the symbols, had for the city of Pawtucket a secular purpose, i.e., to depict the historical origins of a national holiday.[69] The court argues that this is not markedly different from the inclusion of a display of religious art in the National Gallery. Burger does not find evidence that the creche represents a disguised attempt by public officials to propagate a religious view.[70]

Hinging the decision on whether or not the activity under question had a secular purpose would imply a commitment to the Lemon test, the first prong of which is the question of purpose. While Burger's opinion appears to pay homage to this guideline for determining establishment, his commitment to the criterion is provisional enough to catch the attention of Supreme Court watchers.[71] Concluding that the Pawtucket nativity scene indeed had a secular purpose, did not have a primary effect of advancing religion, and did not create excessive government entanglement,[72] Burger, however, expresses the provisional nature of the court's commitment to this test.[73] Nevertheless, if the Lemon test were applied, the city of Pawtucket's creche display would have no problem passing it:

> We are satisfied that the City has a secular purpose for including the creche, that the City has not impermissibly advanced religion, and that including the creche does not create excessive entanglement between religion and government.[74]

In view of the divided nature of the court's opinion on this case, the arguments of the dissenting opinion warrant some consideration. Justice Brennan, whom you will remember wrote a comprehensive concurring opinion in the second major school prayer case (Schempp), wrote a scathing dissent. Brennan charges that the majority's application of the Lemon test was superficial and that the hard-won order of Lemon should not be abandoned.[75]

Brennan argues that it is specious to suggest that the religious significance of the nativity symbols are rendered inconsequential by the secular purpose behind its use.[76] Further, congressional recognition of Christmas as a national holiday does not imply the acceptability of governmental endorsement of the sectarian aspects of it.[77] Maintaining that a nativity scene is an essentially Christian symbol, the religious significance of which cannot be expunged, Brennan argues that its inclusion represents official sanction of a particular religious belief.[78] Apparently basing his argument on the avoidance of religio-political strife theme of Madison, Brennan finds the implied governmental sanction of Christianity in the public display of a creche to violate establishment principles.[79] Our Constitution allows the churches and religious institutions, not government officials, to retain our religious heritage. In conclusion, Brennan argues that the action of the city of Pawtucket is "a coercive, though perhaps small, step toward establishing the sectarian preferences of the majority at the expense of the minority, accomplished by placing public facilities and funds in support of the religious symbolism and theological tidings that the creche conveys."[80]

While I do not presume to articulate what the Supreme Court has been unable to refine in a century of First Amendment cases, that is, an unambivalent overarching principle behind the religion clauses, it seems to me that both clauses do address a concern common to contemporary Protestants as well as Catholics—religious liberty.[81] The prominence of religious liberty as a Roman Catholic concern is highlighted by the "Declaration of Religious Freedom" of Vatican II, although the basis in the dignity of the human person may not be theologically compatible with Protestantism's more pessimistic view of human nature. Allowing for different bases for the theological concern for religious liberty, there is evidence that contemporary Christians are united in their commitment to the value of religious freedom. The Constitution reflects a similar concern.

The establishment clause, insofar as it prohibits governmental favoritism of one religious belief or sect over another, protects minority views from a governmentally created disadvantage. The free exercise clause, insofar as it prevents government from impinging on the right of religious persons to practice their beliefs, obviously protects religious liberty. Of course, there are specific limits to the actualization of these overarching principles, which provide the Supreme Court with complex decisions requiring subtle distinctions. However, it is this rudimentary concern with religious liberty and not preference for secularism that seems to me usually to provide the impetus to the First Amendment decisions I examined. National interests appear to be best served by preserving the national commitment to religious liberty rather than the religious commitment to a national presence for Christianity.

As a brief appendix, I thought it would be helpful to summarize the instances of governmental aid to religion, usually involving church-related education, found constitutionally acceptable in recent years. Justice Burger provides an itemization in *Lynch v. Donnelly:* (1) public money for textbooks used in parochial schools *(Board of Education v. Allen),* (2) public money for transportation of students to parochial schools *(Everson v. Board of Education)*, (3) federal grants for college buildings in church-related institutions, (4) non-categorical grants for church-related colleges, and (5) exemption of church property from taxation *(Walz v. Tax Commission)*.[82] Also, released time religious instruction off school property was found allowable for public school children in *Zorach v. Clauson.*

In addition, the reader might want to explore the following recent Supreme Court decisions written after this study: *Wallace v. Jaffree* and *Mueller v. Allen.* The hard-won clarity for determining establishment by means of the Lemon test has been further muddled.

Selected Bibliography

Devins, Neal. "The Supreme Court and Private Schools: An Update," *This World,* Spring/Summer 1984, no. 8.

Howe, Mark De Wolfe. *The Garden and the Wilderness: Religion and Government in American Constitutional History.* Chicago and London: University of Chicago Press, 1965.

West, Ellis. "The Supreme Court and the Conflict Between the Principles of Religious Liberty and Separation of Church and State." Ph.D. diss., Emory University, 1971, University Microfilms.

_____. "The Supreme Court and Religious Liberty in the Public Schools," *Journal of Church and State,* vol. 25, Winter 1983, pp. 87-112.

Notes

1. Ellis West, "The Supreme Court and the Conflict Between the Principles of Religious Liberty and Separation of Church and State," Ph.D. diss., Emory University, 1971, University Microfilms, p. 3.

2. Milton R. Konvitz, *Expanding Liberties* (New York: Viking Press, 1966), p. 7.

3. Ibid., p. 8. Jefferson's famous phrase appears in a letter to the Danbury Baptist Association.

4. Mark De Wolfe Howe, *The Garden and the Wilderness: Religion and Government in American Constitutional History* (Chicago and London: University of Chicago Press, 1965), p. 19.

5. Ibid.

6. Ibid., p. 2.

7. Ibid., p. 9.

8. Roger Williams, "Mr. Cotton's Letter Lately Printed, Examined and Answered," in *Roger Williams: His Contribution to the American Tradition* (1953), cited by Mark De Wolfe Howe, *Garden and the Wilderness,* p. 6.

9. Howe, *Garden and the Wilderness,* p. 11.

10. James C. Kirby, Jr., "Everson to Meek to Roemer: From Separation to Detente in Church-State Relations," *North Carolina Law Review* 55 (1976–77): 563-75.

11. Ibid., p. 568.

12. Henry J. Abraham, "The Status of the First Amendment Religion Clauses: Some Reflections on Lines and Limits," *Journal of Church and State* 22 (Spring 1980): 215-31.

13. Konvitz, *Expanding Liberties,* p. 3.

14. West, "Supreme Court and the Conflict," p. 22.

15. Konvitz, *Expanding Liberties,* p. 12.

16. Abraham, "Status of the Religion Clauses," p. 218.

17. *Wisconsin v. Yoder,* 406 U.S. 211 (1972).

18. *Wisconsin v. Yoder,* 406 U.S. 209 (1972).

19. *Wisconsin v. Yoder,* 406 U.S. 214 (1972).

20. *Wisconsin v. Yoder,* 406 U.S. 219 (1972).

21. Ibid.

22. Jesse H. Choper, *The Supreme Court: Trends and Developments 1981–1982* (Minneapolis: National Practice Institute, 1983), p. 60.

23. Ibid., p. 58.

24. Ibid.

25. Ibid., p. 60.

26. Abraham, "Status of the Religion Clauses," p. 225.

27. *Zorach v. Clauson,* 343 U.S. 313, 314 (1952). Justice Douglas moved away from this position of accommodation to religion (Konvitz, *Expanding Liberties,* p. 25).

28. Kirby, "Everson to Meek to Roemer," p. 564.

29. Ibid.

30. *Everson v. Board of Education,* 330 U.S. 3 (1946).

31. *Everson v. Board of Education,* 330 U.S. 15, 16 (1946).

32. *Everson v. Board of Education,* 330 U.S. 16 (1946).

33. *Everson v. Board of Education,* 330 U.S. 17 (1946).

34. *Everson v. Board of Education,* 330 U.S. 16 (1946).

35. *Everson v. Board of Education,* 330 U.S. 24 (1946).

36. *Zorach v. Clauson,* 343 U.S. 309 (1951).

37. Kirby, "Everson to Meek to Roemer," p. 565.

38. *Zorach v. Clauson,* 343 U.S. 314 (1951).

39. Louis H. Pollak, "The Supreme Court, 1962 Term, Forward: Public Prayers in Public Schools," *Harvard Law Review* 77 (November 1963): 62-78.

122   PARTNERS IN PEACE AND EDUCATION

40. *Engel v. Vitale,* 370 U.S. 422, 423 (1961).

41. *Engel v. Vitale,* 370 U.S. 425 (1961).

42. *Engel v. Vitale,* 370 U.S. 431 (1961).

43. *Engel v. Vitale,* 370 U.S. 428 (1961).

44. *Engel v. Vitale,* 370 U.S. 445 (1961).

45. *Abington School Dist. v. Schempp,* 374 U.S. 205 (1962).

46. *Abington School Dist. v. Schempp,* 374 U.S. 207 (1962).

47. West, "The Supreme Court and Religious Liberty in the Public Schools," *Journal of Church and State* 25 (Winter 1983): 95.

48. *Abington School Dist. v. Schempp,* 374 U.S. 226 (1962). "While the Free Exercise clause clearly prohibits the use of state action to deny the rights of free exercise to anyone, it has never meant that the majority could use the machinery of the State to practice its belief."

49. Pollak, "The Supreme Court, 1962 Term, Forward," p. 69.

50. *Abington School Dist. v. Schempp,* 374 U.S. 269 (1962).

51. *Abington School Dist. v. Schempp,* 374 U.S. 312, 313 (1962).

52. The secular vs. religious conflict is more apparent in the Madalyn Murray case joined to Schempp.

53. West, "Supreme Court and Religious Liberty," p. 95.

54. Ibid., p. 96.

55. Ibid., p. 99.

56. Ibid., p. 100.

57. *Abington School Dist. v. Schempp,* 374 U.S. 222 (1962).

58. Rowland L. Young, "Supreme Court Report: Court Upholds City's Nativity Scene Display," *American Bar Association Journal* 70 (May 1984): 120.

59. West, "Supreme Court and Religious Liberty," p. 101.

60. Young, "Supreme Court Report," p. 120.

61. *Lynch v. Donnelly,* U.S. Lawyers' Edition Second, vol. 79, no. 3 (April 13, 1984): 623-45.

62. Ibid., p. 613.

63. Ibid., p. 610.

64. Ibid.

65. Ibid. Italics mine.

66. Ibid.

67. Ibid., p. 611. Italics mine.

68. Ibid.

69. Ibid., p. 615. "The narrow question is whether there is a secular purpose for Pawtucket's display of the creche. The display is sponsored by the City to celebrate the Holiday and to depict the origins of that Holiday. These are legitimate secular purposes."

70. Ibid., p. 614.

71. Rowland Young in "The Supreme Court Report" of the *ABA Journal* (p. 120) wonders whether the Lemon test has been modified.

72. *Lynch v. Donnelly,* 79 L.Ed. 2d, p. 617.

73. Ibid., p. 613.

74. Ibid., p. 617.

75. Ibid., pp. 624-26.

76. Ibid., p. 631.

77. Ibid., p. 633.

78. Ibid., p. 631.

79. Ibid., p. 636.

80. Ibid., p. 644.

81. This insight takes its cue from Ellis West's casting of his discussion of the religion clauses and the public schools in terms of religious liberty.

82. *Lynch v. Donnelly,* 79 L.Ed. 2d, p. 615.

Reformed Views of Religion and the Schools

CORNELIUS PLANTINGA, JR.

Introduction

In the case of religion and the schools we find a sensitive and acutely contemporary test of our Catholic and Reformed/Presbyterian views of church and state. First, this case exemplifies and particularizes many of the knotty conceptual and theological issues in the neighborhood of church, state, and kingdom of God: Whose primary responsibility is it to educate children? In the case of Christian children, how apt are state supported, religiously neutral schools for the training of citizens not only of the nation but also of the kingdom of God? Do neutral schools properly train us for "secular" tasks while homes and churches add on "spiritual" training? How plausible is the secular/spiritual distinction itself? Is educational religious neutrality in any case possible? Desirable? Would the state support religious freedom better by having as little as possible to do with all religions and irreligions or rather by seeking impartially to give them all equal sway in the public arena? Is democratic religious tolerance a greater or lesser value than the striving for Christian truth within our own churches? What is at any rate the relation of tolerance and commitment?

Second, the issue before us might be supposed to generate interesting divergences between Catholic views on the one side and Reformed/Presbyterian views on the other. It is usual in Protestant typologies of church/state theories, for example, to classify Catholic views as "church above state" (or Christ above culture). A somewhat sinister disclosure of Catholic designs on the levers and perhaps treasuries of American education sometimes follows:

> Since parochial education is sponsored both by the Roman Catholic
> Church and sectors of the Protestant Church it is well to distinguish be-

124

tween Roman theory and Protestant theory. The Roman Catholic Church insists that only within its boundaries does Christianity find true expression. It regards itself as the one and only Church. It is affirmed that to it alone have been committed the keys of the Kingdom and that the whole order of redemption, not only on earth but also in purgatory, has been entrusted into its keeping. As over against the state, it presses for the acceptance of its claims and where these claims are accepted it urges that Church stands above the state. This means that where Roman Catholicism is dominant it controls the processes of education. Where it is not dominant it contents itself with the best it can get and bides its time with the hope that eventually its claims will be honored and its demands guaranteed and enforced by the state (RCA, I, p. 2).

The Reformed document that contains this winsome portrait (which, on this point, even its framers now probably relegate to a richly deserved obscurity) goes on to assure us that Reformed Christians see matters more healthily: "If we understand our Reformed tradition the Church stands neither above the state nor against the state but Jesus Christ the Lord places his Church within the state that it may preserve and in measure transform the state." It might be added that in exalting the democratic values of freedom and diversity to be found in public school education the document seems to accent preservation and only concede transformation. But, as we shall see, this is by no means the only Reformed emphasis—and I should argue that it is not even the most consistent.

Third, Americans have recently been much agitated by a welter of questions in the area we are considering. Beyond such visible and particular issues as prayer in public schools is a general uneasiness— amounting in some cases to disillusionment—about the course of public education. The PCUSA could say in the "Father Knows Best" era that "public education unfettered by restrictive theological positions or secular ideologies is consonant with the nature of Christian growth" (PCUSA, p. 8). The report then advises us that public school educators "have assured the public" that no such ideologies are present—that in fact the "moral and spiritual values" taught in public schools "are consonant with the principles enunciated by our religious heritage" (ibid., p. 12).

Today, as we all know, doubts have arisen on this score. In an incisive *Reformed Journal* article, Charles Glenn, Director of Equal Educational Opportunity, Massachusetts Department of Education, concedes that the "values clarification" strategy of public schools is philosophically and practically at odds with every revealed religion. It accepts only such moral values as are empirically derived and validated and, further, are thus validated relative to their holder (Glenn, pp. 12, 13). The fact is that declining public school enrollments, choices of alternative schools, values clarification disputes, court cases over the disestablishment of prayers and the establishment of secular humanism are all symptomatic of a broadly religious crisis in American education. Americans do not agree on any basic philosophy of life or ultimate concern, and many are increasingly wary of the particular philosophy the state instantiates in its schools.

Perhaps the most beguiling spectacle in this regard is the flight of Christian fundamentalists from public schools. Fiercely patriotic, many of them, and devoutly Christian, they have found their interests in civil religion increasingly betrayed by a public school system whose religion is no longer even bloodlessly theistic, let alone Protestant, and whose values clarifications seem increasingly uncivil. Hence the emergence of red, white, and blue Christian schools.

I. Relevant Reformed Theological Principles and Their Application

From a Reformed perspective, what particular theological principles apply to the sorts of issues mentioned above? In an earlier paper for our meetings I suggested several that apply broadly to the church's interest in the socio-political world. Let me now reiterate and particularize a couple of these, and then add a third that seems apt for the specific issue of religion and the schools.

First, Reformed people share with many other Christians a conviction that the broadest and most inclusive category of our relation to God is that of kingdom. Sometimes expressed as the "sovereignty of God" principle, or, perhaps subordinately, the "lordship of Christ," the idea here is that no square inch of the universe is unclaimed by God and his Christ. Covenant, church, schools, states, families and marriages, economic institutions—in fact all orders and institutions, all human functions and interests serve, or ought to serve, as instruments of the kingdom.

The concept of religion is accordingly broadened to include not only cultic and cultural patterns of devotional practice and doctrinal belief, but also one's ultimate commitment, one's non-negotiable orientation to God in the whole width and breadth, height and depth, of one's existence. In this respect all of life is religion:

> To be a Christian is not just to accept certain dogmatic beliefs, not just to cultivate certain spiritual feelings, not just to engage in certain acts of worship. It is to be a disciple of Christ in all one's life, for this age and the next. The gospel of Christ speaks to our "secular" and "natural" existence as well as to our "religious" and "spiritual" existence. It speaks to our whole existence—to the whole framework of our beliefs, to the whole complex of our feelings and attitudes, to the whole pattern of our actions . . . So [the Christian] does not seek to renounce all "secular" activities and to withdraw into some special area of the "religious." Nor does he see in these activities a neutral clearing fenced off to faith. Rather, he sees in them all a means of exercising obedient trust in Christ (Wolterstorff, pp. 9-10).

I should concede at once that Reformed Christians, if they might agree broadly with the sovereignty or kingdom principle above, diverge on the question of what it means for education. Within the range of churches represented in our own colloquium, Presbyterians traditionally have supported public education with enthusiasm and have looked with mixed tolerance and annoyance at Christian private and parochial alternative schools. The PCUSA statement cited above, for instance, recognizes (perhaps somewhat grudgingly) the right of private Christian education, but warns repeatedly against the "divisiveness," "sectarianism," "cloistered living," "artificially protected situations," "controlled censorship," "imposition of doctrine," and general undemocratic cussedness in Christian schools. Though one might properly wonder about each of these charges (why, for example, should *imposition* be thought of as the likeliest mode of doctrinal transmission?), the Presbyterian statement means, I think, at least to accept, even if not to champion, the principle of God's sovereignty. It argues, however, that the use and promotion of one state-controlled school system is consonant with this principle. Meanwhile, the PCUSA statement is hostile to the idea that private and parochial Christian schools ought to enjoy any benefits of the tax dollars paid by their adherents, for these schools are in no sense public (PCUSA, p. 20).

The Christian Reformed Church, on the other hand, strongly advocates the use of parentally operated Christian elementary and secondary schools. This is done as a strategic implication of the kingdom principle. That is, if one holds that in some more or less specifiable ways the Christian faith as commitment, as life philosophy, affects our views of such things as the sanctions for moral values, the meaning and interpretation of literature and history, proper attitudes on earthkeeping, the reasons for human individual and collective worth, and so on, then the relevance of the faith for the whole range of educational concerns ought to be taught to our children. It is then a strategic choice whether public education as corrected and supplemented by homes and churches is sufficient for this task. Most, though not all, CRC parents believe that such correcting and supplementing is necessary. For most believe that public school education has a different (and competing) philosophy of life from their own. But since these busy days few of us have time or competence to do all the correcting and supplementing ourselves, we hire teachers and set up Christian schools to do it.

The Reformed Church in America report (written the same year as that of the PCUSA) expresses an intermediate view. The use and support of Christian schools may be advisable for some Christians under some circumstances ("where public education is morally and spiritually detrimental"), but generally it is not, for separate Christian schools tend to breed an unwholesome provincialism, "restrictive absolutism," and intolerance (RCA, III, p. 8; II, p. 4). Further, the report mistakenly supposes that the purpose of Christian schools is to induce children to make a personal confession of faith upon maturity (rather than, say, to produce Christianly educated citizens of the kingdom). It then somewhat perplexingly and blood-warmingly concludes that "to say that parochial schools are essential is to rob Divine grace of its sovereignty. It is to say that God's grace cannot operate without human assistance. It ultimately lands us in the Pope's bailiwick" (RCA, V, p. 1).

Shorn of confessional tendentiousness (which, on other topics, can be more than matched in my own denomination's documents of the same period) the idea here seems to be that there is more than one way to train children for adult Christian lives. This interpretation is confirmed by the RCA statement's later treatment of the kingdom theme. Expectedly, the doctrine of the kingdom is warmly endorsed. But what gets accepted is the biblical theme that though we are not of the world we are in it. In fact, to extend God's claim over every area of life means fight, not flight. It means becoming "immersed in the structures of society"; it means "involvement in [society's] unredeemed life." Here the theme emerges that we have a kingdom mission in public education. Though the nature of this mission is not defined, the general drift of the argument seems clear: Calvinists believe in world service, not world flight. If in the case of public schools this may be dangerous for tender-aged missionaries, we must believe that God will watch over them (RCA V, pp. 7, 8).

Here as between, say, RCA and CRC positions there seems to be no real difference on principle, but rather on strategy for carrying out the dictates of principle. Both Reformed communions (joined by PCUSA, pp. 7, 10, and other Reformed bodies) believe that parents have a responsibility to see that their children are Christianly educated. Some Reformed people (the majority) think this can be done adequately by public schools as corrected and supplemented by home and church. Others (the minority) think it cannot. Both views include the conviction that Christians must be educated to serve as kingdom citizens amid all the blood, smoke, and ambiguity of this world. This is our vocation. Some (the majority) believe there is no time like the present to begin. Hence even first graders belong in public schools. Others (the minority) believe in the need for some years of training toward Christian maturity before the task is undertaken. The question is something like this: Does one learn to swim against the tide by walking into the ocean or by beginning with dry land drills and instruction? Should one learn one's driving on a practice range or in traffic (or on a golf course)?

So far, as suggested, Reformed people differ on strategy. However, there may be two principal disagreements in the sovereignty area as well. (1) Some Reformed people believe (as Wolterstorff in the quotation above) that religious neutrality in all but a few areas of education is impossible. One's worldview, one's religion as ultimate commitment, influences one's interpretation of (even one's interest in) most data of significance in academe. Such Reformed people further believe that the sacred/secular dichotomy is mostly false and misleading. Other Reformed people assert both that educational neutrality is a widespread academic possibility (RCA V, p. 8) and that public schools achieve such neutrality to an acceptable degree. Still further, neutrality proponents are confident that public schools properly "confine themselves to the task of preparing the young to participate in the area of life which may be termed the secular" (RCA II, p. 4).

(2) While all Reformed people believe that a root sin is the tendency to worship the creature rather than the Creator, there is diver-

gence in perception of this danger within public school education and (for that matter) within non-public school education (where there may be temptations to pride). Some Reformed people (the majority) celebrate the homogenizing and democratizing achievements of the public school. Like James Conant, these Reformed Christians see the public school as the mighty "engine of democracy," or as "the greatest bulwark of democracy" (RCA II, p. 3); it alone preserves us from the imposition on us of "sectarian" teaching (PCUSA, *passim*). Other Reformed people (the minority) get very uneasy about all this talk of engines and bulwarks against sectarianism. Let me see (as a sharer of the minority view) if I can state the uneasiness with requisite fairness and delicacy: the impression one sometimes gets in reading certain Reformed or Presbyterian (and surely other denominational) celebrations of the public schools' contribution to democracy is that American democracy is somehow an equal, or even superior, partner with the Christian faith. That is, when one reads the public schools either (1) melt down religious differences to a common denominator theism or, nowadays, generic humanism, or (2) bring into the public arena a multitude of faiths and unfaiths, arranged in a brilliant kaleidoscope for our mutual delectation—when one reads hymns of praise to either of these phenomena one wonders whether human togetherness (perhaps accompanied by what private and essentially marginal religion one likes) has not become more important to us than the gospel of Jesus Christ.

An example from another confessional locus: in the March 21, 1979, memorandum of the Joint ADL-NCCB-USCC Working Study Group (issued by Gene Fisher and Rabbi Leon Klenicki) Dr. Eleanor Blumenberg states that "in many segments of the Jewish Community there is a deep-held fear of the particularism in Catholic moral education which they feel teaches, at least by influence, that those who are not Catholics have less valid value systems and beliefs" (document's paraphrase).

My initial response to such statements is quiet consternation. Is preferring one's own value systems and beliefs over those which disagree with them not a merely inevitable accompaniment of taking such things seriously? Or of being Catholic? Or Jewish? And would a public celebration of the equal validity of all beliefs and value systems (like, say, a celebration of all socioeconomic beliefs) not amount to a trivializing of all those beliefs and a betrayal of one's own? After all, religions, I take it, differ from races, sexes, and ethnic cuisines by making truth claims.

The upshot of these last remarks is that a minority Reformed inclination is to be suspicious of the public school veneration of American democracy *where an implication of such veneration is a relativizing, marginalizing, or trivializing of religious belief.* What puts this segment of the Reformed community on alert is any suggestion that our common Americanism is somehow more significant than our (additional and merely private) religious identities.

So the principle of the sovereignty of God, variously applied to religion and the schools, is one focus of interest. Within the scope of this principle, as we have seen, is a second: the principle of world-formative responsibility (also variously applied) rather than world-flight. (Both these principles are discussed in my earlier paper.)

Let me now add a third (with a sub-idea or two). Though Calvin himself preserved the medieval heritage of a sacral society, his successors have exalted the ideal of freedom of religion within a society that freely permits it. For if one is conscientiously responsible to be a world-formative servant as well as a believer of Christian beliefs and a performer of Christian acts of devotion, then one will hope and work for a society (and a state within it) that permits and even encourages such freedom.

But although all Reformed people would probably endorse this principle *überhaupt,* there is once more considerable disagreement as to what it means for religion and the schools. A majority idea (e.g., PCUSA and RCA statements) is that society's unity and harmony is best maintained by protecting religious freedom, which, in turn, is "best maintained through a continuing allegiance to a free public school system" (PCUSA, p. 5). For only the public school "is devoted to freedom and liberty in the field of religion and religious education" (RCA II, p. 3). Private and parochial schools may also be granted existence, but it is wise to note that they are inherently divisive and it is essential to insure that their adherents continue to pay extra for them.

Here several ideas come together. One is a tendency to see the state as the proper *provider* of such services as education—not just the promoter of them. No doubt this idea fits together with the other one above, namely, that the state's unity and harmony is best served by finding within public schools some common ground on which we can all stand, relegating religious differences to private spheres. Another is to see public education as neutral enough or value-free enough to be a suitable instrument (provided it is supplemented by home and church) for training Christians. Possibly the sacred/secular distinction fits here, too: schools train us for the secular areas of life; the home and church train us for the sacred sphere.

An alternative (minority) Reformed view (Wolterstorff, McCarthy) is, in my opinion, a more excellent way to see religion and the schools and offers a more plausible concept of freedom. I recommend it, in addition, for its promise as an area of possible Catholic-Reformed/Presbyterian convergence.

II. Possible Convergence?

At the beginning of this paper I suggested that American education is suffering a broadly religious crisis. Part of it has to do with the stripping away of the last remnants of Judeo-Christian *devotion* (prayer, Bible reading). With this stripping away I have real sympathy: banal non-denominational prayers and Bible readings for secularists and believers alike have no point and no place in public schools. But it is the broadly *religious,* or *philosophical,* crisis that is truly interesting and important.

This crisis in fact amounts to what could be called a *quandary* in religion and public education (Oppewal, p. 324). On the one hand the state—both within the public schools and elsewhere—is trying to back away from any dealings whatever with religion. The First Amendment establishment clause consistently has been interpreted as requiring not state impartiality but neutrality where religion is concerned. That is, the government is to be isolated from, insulated against, wholly unentangled in, anything called religion.

On the other hand, the courts and other civil agencies have been steadily broadening the definition of religion. In *Torcaso v. Watkins* (1961), for example, the U.S. Supreme Court held that belief in a Supreme Being was not necessary for a system of beliefs to constitute a religion: ethical culture and secular humanism were mentioned as examples. In *Seeger v. United States* (1965) the court took a similar view.

A meeting between the two governmental forces generates a quandary:

Public school policy makers, whether courts or school boards, will be

increasingly forced to choose either (1) to cut educational policy free
from all [religious/philosophical] value commitments and sanctions, or
(2) to take sides, aligning policy with some of the competing value systems rather than others. To adopt either of these alternatives is to court
educational and social disaster. To attempt the first is to attempt to cut
out the heart of education, leaving only the dry husks of facts without
framework, skills without schema. This could never be acceptable to a
serious educator of whatever philosophical orientation. To pursue seriously the second is to return to an era of established religion, an "official" value system by which decisions in education are made and in
which children are steeped. This has always been unacceptable to the
courts and to most Americans (Oppewal, p. 324).

I believe the second alternative has in fact been chosen in American public education and that it is just this that has precipitated the
broadly religious crisis mentioned above. In values clarifications the
only legitimate sanctions are non-theistic. In textbook content religion
is not a significant or molding force. (It is therefore possible for public
school civics books to treat the whole 1955–56 Montgomery boycott
and its relation to the civil rights movement without ever mentioning
that Martin Luther King, Jr., was a pastor or that black churches were
the centers of the movement.) Some secondary biology textbooks are
not consistent with theistic understandings of the data in question—as
is acknowledged by some of their supporters as well as detractors (Wendell Bird, pp. 521-22).

If indeed the public schools are inculcating non-theism by elimination, that is, by removing theism from any significant place as a
mover and shaker of human life, and if in fact they are affirmatively inculcating some form of generic humanism by suggesting that the scientific method is the only proper truth validator, or that revelation as a
means to the same end is untrustworthy, or the like, then the state ought
either to (1) cut off tax dollars to every school system on the ground
that no one of them—including the public one—can avoid inculcating
some values or other (ones unacceptable to other citizens), or else (2)
fund all school systems, openly recognizing that Americans differ on
questions of religion and irreligion and that no one system ought to be
preferred to another (McCarthy, p. 134).

Even if the public schools are *not* guilty of affirmatively inculcating secular humanism, even if they are succeeding in embracing the
first horn of the dilemma above (i.e., teaching without inculcating any

philosophical or religious values whatever), then some of America's citizens are still educationally unfree—namely all the ones who think education *ought* to be in a valuational context, such as a Christian one. These citizens are financially coerced: they cannot get state-mandated education for their children in a way that satisfies their conscience without paying extra for it. They thus suffer discrimination as surely as if the state offered medicaid and medicare only for treatment by accupuncture, inviting dissenting patients to take it or leave it, that is, to use this state-supported approach to medicine or else exercise their medical freedom by paying for alternative methods themselves.

The point is that if the state *can* achieve its purpose in education (seeing to it that all citizens are, so far as possible, minimally educated) without discriminating religiously among its citizens, then it ought to do so. For the state ought to allow, and even promote, as much freedom of religion as it can. And this includes, beyond worship and belief, the freedom to express one's religious commitment, one's life philosophy, in education (Wolterstorff, p. 36).

But *can* the state allow freedom of religion educationally not only for non-valuationists (if there be such) and secular humanists, but also for Amish, Catholics, Baptists, militant atheists, Lutherans, Muslim— yea even for the Reformed?

It can. As one of my brothers repeatedly reminds me, where a quandary or dilemma is concerned (as above) there is a maneuver known to theologian and matador alike as "escaping between the horns." In the present case such escape means abandoning the impossible, and in any case discriminatory, concept of state neutrality with respect to religion, and affirming instead the genuinely pluralistic concept of state *impartiality* as among all religions and irreligions. On this view the state would make no vain attempt to isolate itself from all competing values, philosophies, and religions in the marketplace. It would no longer through its courts present such ludicrous spectacles as deciding that secular textbooks do not advance religious ideas but wall maps do. Surely it would not pretend that it may never *de facto* aid any religion or irreligion (never put out church fires, say, or keep peace at atheist meetings). Nor would the state establish by tax funds or by any other method some *one* religion or irreligion. It would rather allow them all free exercise. It would give them all equal sway—in freedom of assembly and speech, in access to the tax dollar, and in every other relevant way (Wolterstorff, pp. 36, 38, and *passim*).

State impartiality in a truly pluralist society is a better guarantor of religious liberty than we now possess and is therefore more consonant with democratic values. Some states (certain Canadian provinces, Israel, the Netherlands, England, Belgium) already exhibit such a vision and method. Because impartiality in a pluralist society offers *genuine* religious freedom, because it handles growing religious and philosophical diversity within such societies as the U.S. (we are at least as much a nation of nations as a melting pot), because it hedges against civil religion, because it rightly sees the state as a proper promoter, but not provider, of education, this is an idea whose time has come.

Works Cited

Bird, Wendell. "Freedom of Religion and Science Instruction in Public Schools." *Yale Law Journal* 78 (1978): 504-26, cited in McCarthy et al., p. 125.

Glenn, Charles L. "Can We Stop Fighting Over Religion and Public Education?" *Reformed Journal* 34 (June 1984).

McCarthy, Rockne, Donald Oppewal, Walfred Peterson, and Gordon Spykman. *Society, State, and Schools.* Grand Rapids: Wm. B. Eerdmans, 1981.

Oppewal, Donald. "Religion and Public Education: An Emerging Quandary." *Educational Forum* (March 1967): 323-31.

Presbyterian Church in the United States of America. *The Church and the Public Schools.* Philadelphia: Board of Education of the PCUSA, 1957.

Reformed Church in America. "Report of the Committee on Educational Philosophy to the 1957 Synod." Mimeographed.

Wolterstorff, Nicholas. *Religion and the Schools.* Grand Rapids: Wm. B. Eerdmans, 1965.

Selected Bibliography

I. Primary Sources

A. Catholic:

The Challenge of Peace: God's Promise and our Response. A Pastoral On War and Peace. May 3, 1983. National Conference of Catholic Bishops. Washington, D.C.: United States Catholic Conference, 1983.

Flannery, Austin, ed. *Vatican Council II. The Conciliar and Post-Conciliar Documents.* Grand Rapids, Mich.: Wm. B. Eerdmans, 1984. The documents most pertinent to our conversations are the Pastoral Constitution on the Church in the Modern World *(Gaudium et spes)* and the Declaration on Christian Education *(Gravissimum educationis)*. Another foundational document is Pope John XXIII's *Pacem in Terris*.

To Teach as Jesus Did. Washington, D.C.: United States Catholic Conference, 1972.

Teach Them: A Statement Issued by the Catholic Bishops of the United States May 6, 1976. Pastoral Letters, 1975–1983. Washington, D.C.: United States Catholic Conference, 1984. Pp. 148-56.

B. Presbyterian/Reformed:

Calvin, John. *Institutes of the Christian Religion.* Philadelphia: Westminster, 1960.

Christian Faith and the Nuclear Arms Race: A Reformed Perspective. New York: Reformed Church in America, 1980.

The Church, the Public School, and Creation-Science. In *Minutes 195th General Assembly Presbyterian Church (U.S.A.) 1983. Part I.* New York: Office of the General Assembly, 1984.

Cochrane, Arthur C., ed. *Reformed Confessions of the 16th Century.* Philadelphia: Westminster, 1966.

Dowey, Edward A., ed. *A Commentary on the Confession of 1967 and an Introduction to The Book of Confessions.* Philadelphia: Westminster, 1968.

Peacemaking: The Believers' Calling. The United Presbyterian Church in the United States of America. New York: General Assembly of the United Presbyterian Church in the USA, 1980.

"Religion and Public Education." In *Digest of the Proceedings of the General Assembly of the Presbyterian Church U.S.* Pp. 232-45.

Rogers, Jack, ed. *Presbyterian Creeds: A Guide to the Book of Confessions.* Philadelphia: Westminster, 1985.

II. Secondary Sources

Carper, James C., and Thomas C. Hunt, eds. *Religious Schooling in America.* Birmingham, Ala.: Religious Education Press, 1984.

Daum, Annette, and Eugene Fisher, eds. *The Challenge of Shalom for Catholics and Jews: A Dialogical Discussion Guide to the Catholic Bishops Pastoral on Peace and War.* New York: Union of American Hebrew Congregations in Cooperation with the National Conference of Catholic Bishops, 1985.

Devins, Neal. "The Supreme Court and Private Schools: An Update." *This World* 8 (1984): 13-26.

Dwyer, Judith, ed. *The Catholic Bishops and Nuclear War. A Critique and Analysis of the Pastoral The Challenge of Peace.* Washington, D.C.: Georgetown University Press, 1984.

Harrington, Daniel J. *God's People in Christ: New Testament Perspectives on the Church and Judaism.* Philadelphia: Fortress, 1980.

Johnson, James T. *Can Modern War Be Just?* New Haven: Yale University Press, 1984.

_____. *Just War Tradition and the Restraint of War: A Moral and Historical Inquiry.* Princeton, N.J.: Princeton University Press, 1981.

McCarthy, Rockne et al. *Society, State, and Schools.* Grand Rapids: Wm. B. Eerdmans, 1981.

Murnion, Philip J., ed. *Catholics and Nuclear War: A Commentary on The Challenge of Peace. The U.S. Catholic Bishops' Pastoral Letter on War and Peace.* New York: Crossroad, 1983. Distributed by Winston Press, Minneapolis, Minn.

Murray, John C. *We Hold These Truths: Catholic Reflections on the American Proposition.* New York: Sheed and Ward, 1960.

Niebuhr, Reinhold. *The Nature and Destiny of Man: A Christian Interpretation*. New York: Scribner's, 1953.

Pawlikowski, John T., and Donald Senior, eds. *Biblical and Theological Reflections on "The Challenge of Peace."* Wilmington, Del.: Michael Glazier, 1984.

Peace Studies Newsletter. Seton Hall University. 3/1 (1984). A bibliography.

Sizer, Theodore R., ed. *Religion and Public Education*. Boston: Houghton Mifflin, 1967.

Stackhouse, Max L. "An Ecumenist's Plea for a Public Theology." *This World* 8 (1984): 47-79.

Stone, Ronald H., ed. *Reformed Faith and Politics*. Washington, D.C.: University Press of America, 1983.

Walzer, Michael. *Just and Unjust Wars: A Moral Argument with Historical Illustrations*. New York: Basic Books, 1977.

_____. *The Revolution of the Saints: A Study in the Origins of Radical Politics*. Cambridge, Mass.: Harvard University Press, 1965.

Wolterstorff, Nicholas. *Educating for Responsible Action*. Grand Rapids: Wm. B. Eerdmans, 1980.

Partners in Peace and Education: Discussion Questions

Session #1. *Purpose:* **Getting to know each other in our shared and differing experiences.**

1. What is it like to be a Catholic? A Presbyterian or Reformed? Please answer by sharing one or two of your most meaningful church experiences.

2. What are some of the common Presbyterian/Reformed perceptions of Catholics? Catholic perceptions of Presbyterians and Reformed? How valid are these?

3. Share some of your family stories about experiences with other Christian groups in America.

4. What role do you feel Catholics have played in American society? Presbyterians and Reformed?

Read for Session #2: Introduction, "Theological Context" of the joint statement.

Session #2. *Purpose:* **To understand the biblical and theological bases of our churches' involvement in society.**

1. How do we understand the kingdom of God? In the present? In the future?

2. What does the document mean when it says that the church "lives its life against the horizon of the kingdom"? Are the church and the kingdom the same?

3. History has taught us both the limitations and possibilities in our understandings of the kingdom of God. Examples are the medieval papal states, Geneva under John Calvin, and the issue of a "National Church" in Hitler's Germany. How do such experiences help us to respond to contemporary issues and events?

4. The document suggests that we have today "greater opportunities and responsibilities with respect to our government and our society" than the first Christians had in the early church. Why and how?

The first two questions in Session #3 will need some preparation. You may want to use the bibliography (pp. 136-38) for your reflections.

Session #3. *Purpose:* To share together the historical and contemporary roles of the churches in American society.

1. Both the Catholic and Presbyterian/Reformed traditions have occupied prominent places in shaping American society. In what ways are the roles of Catholics and Reformed in America changing today?

2. What do you believe are the best ways the churches should influence society on peace, education, or other issues?

3. How helpful has your church been in educating its members in significant issues such as civil rights, the war in Vietnam, and contemporary economic and social issues?

4. Drawing upon the above discussion, what are some necessary distinctions between church, society, and state?

Read for Session #4 the peace documents included in this book and the "Church and Nuclear Warfare" section of the joint statement.

Session #4. *Purpose:* To compare the official positions of the Catholic and Presbyterian/Reformed churches on peace and war.

1. What are the common and distinctive modes of argument and themes in the various statements?

2. How does each tradition use the Bible in coming to its conclusions? What biblical theme or passage has been most helpful to you personally in confronting issues of peace and war?

3. Four theological motifs are identified at the end of this section of the document as lying behind the discussion on peace and the threat of nuclear war. Select one theme and in groups of three speak about it in terms of your belief and experience.

4. The document suggests that we need to learn from each other to insure that we embrace both the inner and outer dimensions of peacemaking. Between inner and outer, choose the dimension you are *least* comfortable with and discuss with others of similar discomfort.

Session #5. *Purpose:* To explore three options confronting Christians in a nuclear age: traditional pacifism, just war, and nuclear pacifism.

1. In our time pacifism ("non-violence") has emerged as a major option facing the churches. No longer is it the exclusive position of the so-called Peace Churches in Protestantism or of small groups within Catholicism such as the followers of Dorothy Day. Why has this change come about? What are the contributions and limitations of pacifism to peacemaking?

2. The possibility of legitimate coercion between nations is discussed throughout the documents. The just war theory has been central to such discussions. Is this theory still applicable in today's world?

3. Given the reality that "in modern life, the instruments of coercive power reach devastating proportion," many people propose "nuclear pacifism." Do you think this option is workable in the light of the complex relations between nations today?

4. Discuss any other options members of the group may wish to share.

Read for Session #6 the section of the joint document on "Church and School" and papers by Burtchaell, Hickey, and Plantinga.

Session #6. *Purpose:* To discover the reasons behind our often differing attitudes toward educational issues and to explore ways of cooperating to ensure the quality of American education.

1. Both traditions have strong commitments to education. In what ways does education lead us to appreciate God's creation and to learn how to live and serve each other as sisters and brothers?

2. Catholics and Presbyterian/Reformed have had different experiences historically in America with the public school system. How have our experiences shaped the way we approach current issues of debate regarding education?

3. Participants from both traditions have expressed concern that in the guise of "neutrality" the religious contribution to society as well as religious viewpoints are excluded from the public schools, while antireligious viewpoints are at times set forth. How do you see the problem and what are some solutions?

4. Although teaching "about" religion has in the past two decades become part of the curriculum of nearly all public colleges and universities, in grades 1-12 children are educated with virtually no exposure to the great faith traditions. What possibilities do you see for teaching about religion in the public schools?

Read for Session #7: "Challenges Ahead" from the document.

Session #7. *Purpose:* To conclude the discussion on education and to summarize how churches can become partners in peace and education.

1. Arguments for and against tax relief have been presented. This subject makes a good topic for debate. Please be sure that some persons choose to debate on a side contrary to their actual position.

2. Do you see a style of witness in either peace or education in the other tradition that would be helpful in your own church?

3. In light of this experience together and the "Challenges Ahead" section of the document, how would you see your congregations cooperating with each other in your community?

PARTNERS IN PEACE AND EDUCATION

Response Form for Discussion Groups

1. Name of discussion group (please list congregation/parishes involved):

_____

_____

2. Dates discussion group met: _____

3. Did you use the Discussion Questions included in *Partners in Peace and Education*? Yes____ No____

A. If you did not, what format did you follow? _____

_____

_____

B. If you did, please answer the following questions:

    1. How many weeks did you meet? _____

    2. Was this length of time: too short ____ too long ____ just right ____ ?

    3. Where did you meet? _____

    4. What was the average attendance? _____

4. What were the major learnings in your discussion groups? _____

_____

_____

_____

_____

5. What suggestions do you have in making this kind of volume more useful for future church education? _____

_____

_____

6. What future plans emerged from your discussion group for further ecumenical and education ventures? _____

_____

_____

_____

Please return to: Eugene Fisher
                 Bishop's Committee for Ecumenical and Interreligious Affairs
                 National Conference of Bishops
                 1312 Massachusetts Ave. N.W.
                 Washington, D.C. 20005

DATE DUE